ROSIE'S BACK HOME!
POSITIVE AGEING FOR
A RESTLESS SPIRIT

Rosie Ross

First published 2025
by Rowanvale Books Ltd
The Gate
Keppoch Street
Roath
Cardiff
CF24 3JW
www.rowanvalebooks.com

A CIP catalogue record for this book is available from the British Library.
Paperback ISBN: 978-1-83584-147-1
eBook ISBN: 978-1-83584-146-4

To my dear friends Cathy, Helen, Jenny, Jude, Tracey, Philippa and Jill, for all their support in all its different forms

Contents

Invitation to Share My Experience 11

From Seeds to Synthesis 14

About the Book.. 18

SECTION 1: THE SPIRIT AWAKENS.............................. 23

Rumblings of Discontent 25

From Illness to Insight: A Chain of Events..................... 29

Inspiration Through Conversation 35

Inspiration over a drink 37

Inspiration after book group............................... 37

Inspiration from morose moments........................... 39

Squaring Up to 'Encumbrance':

Today's Secure Anchor, Tomorrow's Ball and Chain?.40

Disencumbering: Facing the Giant 43

Housequandary 45

Moggiemalady 47

FOMO (Fear of Missing Out)........................... 49

Cellomania.. 52

Oldfogeyness and Stagnata 55

The 50% Club... 59

SECTION 2: MAKING IT HAPPEN 63

Whims + Ideas = Honesty! 65

Commitment with Flexibility 70

Kindness and Company, Through Servas 73

Serendipity, Not Anonymity!

Opportunities to Connect 75

The Battle of the Bulge 83

Defeating the Dreaded Packing! 85

Organisation: The Price of Sanity 91

Amazingly, the Big Day Arrives! 97

SECTION 3: INTO THE UNKNOWN 101

Staying Strong 103

People to Appreciate – and Some to Avoid! 107

    Alone but not lonely 108

    Alone and intrepid 112

    Unpredictable, casual encounters 114

    Small-group travel and unchosen company ... 117

Going for It and Managing Risk 120

    Alcohol 121

    Backup plans 122

    Staying safe... Did I? A risk too far? 123

Stuff Matters! 132

    Possessions 132

    Money 133

SECTION 4: TRAVELLING – SOME MAGICAL (AND NOT-SO-MAGICAL) MOMENTS..........................137

British Columbia, Canada: A Welcoming First Stop.139

Vancouver...139

Denman Island 143

Hornby Island...145

The American Southwest: Land of Enchantment and Kindness...149

San Francisco 149

El Capitan 151

The Grand Canyon..152

New Mexico 154

Peru: The Experience! 159

A shaky start 159

A tiny plane over the Nazca Lines..............160

The wonders of Lake Titicaca 161

Rainbow Mountain 164

The Lares Trek – a good decision?.............165

Machu Picchu...168

The Amazon jungle 168

Alone again, with time to reflect.................170

Rapa Nui: A Peaceful Break.................................173

Well, I finally got there!.................................173

Relaxation, 'downtime' and a mistake.....175

French Polynesia 178

    From bad to worse! 178

    Stuck in paradise 182

The Cook Islands: A Little Paradise! 184

    A very different Polynesia 184

    Adventures in Aitutaki 185

    Resting on Rarotonga 187

Australia – Wow! 190

    The Red Centre 192

    Hospitality and drought in New South Wales 197

    Diverse environments 199

    Happy reunions 201

    Getting to know the south 205

    Impressions of Australia 209

New Zealand – and Rain 211

    North Island 211

    South Island 213

    Tourism's highs and lows 219

Guillotine! 222

SECTION 5: READJUSTMENT **227**

Same Town, Very Different Circumstances 229

Uncertainty Remains 233

The Significance of 'Home' 235

Unencumbered After All That?..242

The Journey Continues… 249

The Here and Now 256

POSTSCRIPT: SOME SUGGESTIONS

FOR A POSITIVE EXPERIENCE.......................................**258**

ACKNOWLEDGEMENTS..**269**

Thanks to Local Friends 269

Thanks for Kindness en Route 271

Thanks to 18 Servas Hosts...275

FURTHER READING...**279**

INVITATION TO SHARE
MY EXPERIENCE

On my 67th birthday, I was renting a small bungalow by the sea in Aitutaki, one of the Cook Islands in the South Pacific. Aitutaki is the most remote and exotic place I have ever visited, and it offered me a great sense of adventure.

Early that evening, there was a knock on the door, and outside were three local people with two Lambretta scooters. One pillion seat was free, and I was beckoned over to get on. I had never met the driver, didn't know where we were going, and there were no crash helmets to be seen. I remembered one of the diktats my caring and careful dad imposed on me in my teens: 'You don't EVER ride pillion, even with someone you know well, and if you ever really need to get on a motorbike, you wear a crash helmet!' But fifty years on, I broke the rules. I banished any fear, cocked my leg over, held on tight and was whisked away – literally – into that glorious Cook Islands sunset. What followed was my most-memorable-ever birthday celebration. And I'm still here to tell the tale and cherish the memory!

This book is about the many wonderful and challenging experiences which surrounded that particular event.

My story is about a journey, both physical and emotional. It is a story of adventure, self-discovery, hope and love, and it (so far) has a very happy ending – though I take nothing for granted. I am 71 years young as I write it, starting in the autumn of 2023. It is not a travelogue in the geographical sense but an account of my self-planned psychological experiment, through which I found freedom, excitement and exposure to the possibility of fundamental change.

I am writing because I hope it might be helpful to share my experiences with those of you who, perhaps recently retired or semi-retired, are searching but are not quite sure what for. Perhaps you feel that time is running out for you to do something interesting with your life. Perhaps you still aren't sure what you want your life to look like if and when you finally grow up (which happens very late in life for some of us). Perhaps you just feel that there's got to be more than this. If so, come on – pack your bag and come with me!

If any of my story resonates with you and helps you to find your way forward, or if you simply enjoy reading it, it will have been worth the writing.

FROM SEEDS TO SYNTHESIS

First, there was a strong sense of discontent, a need for change, a desire to do something new, bold, unexpected. I quite fancied travelling, but I had little idea of how, or where to go. Little did I know just what kind of a journey I was embarking on when my feet first took me out of the door and onto a new path. It was far, far more than geographical. I left to go travelling for a year when I was 66, and I wrote a detailed travel blog capturing my various adventures and escapades. Afterwards I wanted to print it and bind it, to share my experiences face to face with friends, and for my own reminiscing. I spent many hours at my computer, editing and improving the blog, but two years later, I was only halfway through and I had lost my enthusiasm – and life in general had taken over. The document languished, neglected, until...

I was contacted in 2023 by the blog platform, asking me to cough up another year's subscription. Jolt of guilt! The email made me realise it was time to decide what to do about my writing, so with renewed, pioneering determination, I did all I could to make sure I had saved (offline) all the raw material. Then, guess what... I set the whole thing aside – again! I just couldn't find the energy to move it forward.

Meanwhile, I read Siobhan Daniels's book *Retirement Rebel*, in which she describes how she left work in her fifties to travel in a mobile home for three years. It's an uplifting book with a strong emphasis on positive ageing, and it fertilised some seeds which were already germinating in my thoughts. Thank you, Siobhan! I am increasingly aware that we live in an ageist society where growing old is often and openly seen as shameful and to be avoided, and often linked with fear. Old age is often associated with mental dysfunction and can involve institutionalised degradation. Women, in particular, can become all but invisible when they get to a certain age. (How many of us have been passed over in a shop or bar while awaiting attention?) For a detailed analysis of modern ageism, see Ashton Applewhite's book *This Chair Rocks: A Manifesto Against Ageism*. She adeptly brings to our attention the seriousness of the problem.

One day, after a windswept walk on Hampsfell, my good friend Philippa and I were enjoying a cup of tea (from leaves in a real teapot) in Grange-over-Sands. I was telling her how much I had learned through using the internet, not only while planning my travels but in many other ways. Philippa suggested that I might want to 'give back to the internet', having taken so much from it. That idea stayed with me.

Thus, this book came about: inspired by Siobhan Daniels and encouraged by Philippa, I decided to use my experiences as the basis for a contribution to the discussion of positive ageing – and that was just the start!

Since then, my ideas have developed. My main purpose in writing this story is to offer ideas, suggestions and caveats to anyone who might be considering a potentially life-changing experience in later life. My plan involved solo travel, but many of the fundamental questions apply in widely differing circumstances and contexts. Rather than offering analysis, checklists and action points, I hope to offer you something more readable. My background, motivation, emotions and personality all affected the course of my experiment and my responses to a range of situations. If you can see where I am coming from, it might help you, yourself, to work out how you might handle similar situations – and you might well view things very differently from me. In adopting this approach, I hope to offer an anecdotal 'self-help' book with a difference. I offer you my story in full; please take from it anything of interest.

ABOUT THE BOOK

In Section 1: 'The Spirit Awakens', I describe how my thought patterns changed (and had to!) to make my adventure possible. Looking closely at the discontent I was feeling required complete honesty; I had to find, by looking at myself, the barriers to change that I had created, and the honesty I found was often uncomfortable. Dismantling the barriers led me to open myself to different approaches to who I am, how I live, and to ways forward that I would never have considered. I began to recognise and seize opportunities where I had never before seen them. This in itself was exciting. Opening myself up enabled me to find new meaning in everyday conversations and to reflect on their implications. My subsection on Disencumbering gives you a far-reaching example of how one word in a conversation can be life-changing.

Section 2: 'Making It Happen' offers insight into how my broad plans became a reality. I emphasise the importance of acknowledging whims and fancies, which are often manifestations of deeper desires. I also stress the importance of commitment to your plan. Because life starts to change once the plan is hatched, and this plan is likely to become your main purpose in life – it's not for dabbling with! I write about the many events (some planned and some serendipitous) which helped me to avoid a sense of isolation. Embarking on a life-changing adventure can feel lonely, and I believe the support and help offered by friends and acquaintances is indispensable for staying sane. I offer many examples of just how this support emerged and how vital it was for my adventure. Whatever your project, physical health is as important as mental well-being, so I include a short section on this. The section concludes with some practical considerations designed to ease the process and minimise stress.

Section 3: 'Into the Unknown' is about survival – sometimes against the odds. Exploring new activities, people and places can be challenging, especially when doing this alone. I believe people gain strength through experience, and I offer examples of how my experiences of travel helped me to find the confidence to go further. Whatever your field of adventure, I believe some prior experience of that same field is useful. I offer you anecdotes about the many ways in which human company varied throughout my travels, and the importance of deciding what type of company I needed at different times, always remembering that I could welcome or reject it. No new experience is risk-free, and I show how I did my best (not always successfully) to calculate and manage the risks which excited and confronted me. Lastly, I explain how I tried to handle my material possessions with minimal stress.

An account of my adventure would not be complete without a description of the various ways in which travel in different countries affected me. That's what Section 4: 'Travelling –Some Magical (and Not-So-Magical) Moments' is. A complete travelogue would be beyond the scope of this book and would distract from my main purpose, so I try to distil the impact of each country I visited on my awareness and on my attitudes. While travel was the 'meat' of my experience, it was only a part of the whole. It was the impact of the travel which mattered.

Section 5: 'Readjustment' is about how life developed after the earlier stages of my adventure. The readjustment was, itself, something of an adventure, and it continues joyfully and constantly. I write about the end of my travels, brought on by the Covid pandemic, and the effects of the pandemic and of my travels on my ability to readjust. I describe the broad-ranging decisions I needed to make, and continue to make, from my renewed perspective on life. And I offer some analysis of whether I have achieved what I set out to, what remains incomplete, and how I hope to sustain the positive outcomes I feel I have achieved. This adventure is not over yet!

SECTION 1: THE SPIRIT AWAKENS

I hope this section illustrates the very gradual process through which my plans emerged, and the importance of being an opportunist. Even if your initial ideas are entirely different from mine, I hope my description of some of the events I experienced, and my reactions to them, will stimulate thought.

RUMBLINGS OF DISCONTENT

One day, as it was going dark, I went back into my house after struggling to mow my too-big lawn full of dandelions and other weeds. I had one of those electric hover mowers with a flex that can easily be cut through. Not only had I been manoeuvring the damn thing, but I had expended many more calories wrapping the flex around where I thought my waist was, then re-winding it around my shoulders, unsuccessfully trying to prevent it going between my legs, then cavorting clumsily to avoid tripping over it. Norman Wisdom couldn't have done it better! My neighbours didn't hide their wry smiles from over the fence – such are the joys of suburban life. I looked out of the window afterwards and spent five seconds complimenting myself on my efforts. Then a lingering question returned: Why do I stay here, too far out of town and with this huge garden? Well, the house was very comfortable and I'd worked hard to make it my own after my ex left – so moving would be a wrench. And I had no idea where I'd move to. So, I stayed.

I had my usual salad meal, then got my cello out, needing to practise for my lesson the next day. I love my cello; its beautiful wood and deep resonance can be very grounding. There is nothing like the cello for reflecting the cellist's state of mind. On this occasion, it just *would not* play in tune, and as I was grumpy from mowing the lawn, my bow kept hitting the wrong strings. My frustration was palpable. Of course, the cello was to blame. Perhaps I should pack in the lessons and just enjoy playing it? Or maybe buy myself a better cello? What was certain was that my cello was not always my best friend and couldn't be relied on to make me happy. Perhaps I should just buy myself an Xbox with all the gear – big telly and a subwoofer? Er, no. Come on, Rosie, you've never played more than Tetris, and you only did that when you were bored! Large-scale retail therapy wasn't a good way to find satisfaction.

These are superficial examples of a deeper discontent which had been with me for several years and had grown stronger with semi-retirement. During my 60s, I was living an outwardly fortunate life: healthy enough, comfortably off, with some wonderful friends, some musical talent and a 'nice' house. But this wasn't enough. The chorus went something like this (violins, please...):

'There's something missing, but I don't know what. My friends are great, but there's no one special. I've got some professional skills, but I want to do something different, and I can't think of any voluntary work I fancy. Lancaster is a great place, but it's not giving me what I need. I sort of feel a bit lost. Time ticks away and something has to change, but I don't know what or how to find out what.'

I was experiencing what Buddhists might call 'samsara' – a cycle of aimless drifting, wandering or a mundane existence. I had done nothing to change this – after all, there were people in far worse situations than me, so shouldn't I just stop whingeing?

Since the noughties, this type of lament had often reared its head, but I hadn't wanted to bore my friends with endless whining and questions about how to make things better. I did raise the topic (well, more than once, I admit), and after raising their eyes to heaven, they all patiently suggested ways forward, but nothing they said really fired me up. I had a few counselling sessions; that didn't work either. All I knew, when I awoke on my 65th birthday in August 2017, was that I was not prepared to wake up at 75 and wonder where the last ten years had gone. As it turned out, that resolution was a driving force, galvanising me to seek change. It became a focus for the remaining months of 2017 and led to some big decisions.

So, I will tell you about my journey, which gradually led me to a way of being that was (and still is, touch wood) happy, fulfilled and optimistic. I had lived with the internal voices that told me to count my blessings and stop thinking like a spoilt brat; there were times when I almost resigned myself to more of the same for ever. And I had made lots of futile attempts at positive thinking (which I've often found myself good at). Systematic planning wasn't an option because I had no idea where or how I wanted to end up; I had even less idea how to get there. So, I opened myself, as totally as I could, to possibility and invited the wind to blow. And in the end, something out there in the universe, along with an opportunistic mindset, helped me find my way. Here's how it happened.

FROM ILLNESS TO INSIGHT: A CHAIN OF EVENTS

Rewind to December 2015, when many people in Lancashire suffered a virulent chest infection. When I succumbed, I remember thinking it was my worst ever. It turned into bronchitis and the GP (probably rightly) refused me antibiotics, so I was tired, weak and in pain for almost a month – not what I needed in the weeks before Christmas. Friends were coming round so that we could cook together on Christmas Day, and I'd bought a duck, but I wanted to hibernate and wake up after Christmas. This is not in my nature, but I really did feel ill. I therefore resolved never to spend another winter in Lancaster, especially in January, which can be dreary. This became an opportunity for me to seek an alternative.

Thanks to seasonal excesses of chocolate and Prosecco, I managed to stagger through Christmas. I had booked to go to Malta in January for the Valletta International Baroque Festival, and I recovered, just enough, in time to go. This was the beginning of a series of events which expanded my horizons and opened me to possibilities. I went to Malta with Cathy (my ex who is now a close friend), Jude (my baroque music buddy) and Liz (a longtime soulmate).

Halfway through a week of terrific baroque music in Valletta we took a day trip to Gozo, a smaller island just a boat ride away. It struck both me and Liz that this could be a place to spend our winters, so we returned to Gozo in April 2016 to investigate further. And whoops... We both fell in love with Gozo! This was the start of a passionate quest for us both. We made some expat friends on Gozo and considered, open-mindedly, various options for spending more time there. We both returned independently to Gozo several times, sometimes renting for a month, sometimes on several shorter visits. I loved spending time with new friends, did some fabulous coastal walks, ate and drank well, had friends over from the UK and enjoyed volunteering at Dreams of Horses, an animal rescue centre. I have fond memories of Gozo's own summer music festival – classical concerts followed by balmy late evenings with friends in outdoor cafés in St George's Square. It was a happy period, and I even considered living there part-time. Liz developed her own links on Gozo, and we sometimes timed our visits to coincide. But ultimately our needs were different: I wanted rugged coastal walks and opportunities to play music with local people; Liz loved the café culture and had a wider interest in the arts, so our relationships with Gozo developed in different directions. Liz returns later in my story.

Gozo was also a place where I found new friends. I was fortunate to meet expat Jill (now living back in the UK). Each time I visited Gozo, we met and I had fun staying with her for a few days. I always enjoyed her company and appreciated her kindness, and since her return to the UK, we have become firm friends. I also made friends with Barbara, an Aussie expat. We enjoyed walks and concerts, and had a lot of fun drinking Aperol Spritz together, subsequently meeting in Valletta for the annual baroque festival. I stayed in her apartment several times. Barbara introduced me to her very kind sister, Joanne, whom I eventually visited in Australia.

But as things turned out, I decided not to make Gozo a winter home. Despite quite an effort on my part, Gozo didn't offer me a way forward as an amateur cellist. I even tried to learn the cornet, a more portable instrument which might qualify me to join one of Gozo's brass bands. That died a death when I was told

I should move on to the tenor horn because my mouth was too big for the cornet! (I have omitted my friends' charming comments about this.) I came to realise that expat communities are, inherently, transient – meaning that friendships can dissolve overnight when someone moves on. This is not my way. Because I have no close family, long-term friendships matter – so this made me question whether I was cut out for expat life. Looking at the established local Gozitan culture, predominantly devout Roman Catholic, I realised this was not for me either, so I couldn't see how I would become part of any Gozo community. I had also learned that Gozo, through its association with Malta, endured more blatant corruption than I was used to in the UK. (How things can change!) Nor could I live on an island where they shoot birds for sport. Lastly, Gozo is a very small island – I needed a bigger world.

However, my Gozo experience was a crucial step in my journey, and I am still very fond of its welcoming atmosphere and its stunning coastline. Meeting the expat community, mainly through walking groups, presented me with the opportunity to question the notion of 'home'. I met people who usually moved on after several years in one country, others who owned a small apartment but lived as international maritime travellers on a boat in the Med. Interestingly, several ageing British expats were about to move back to the UK to be nearer to their grandchildren and the NHS. I also unearthed some juicy comments about one or two expats who were, reportedly, unable to move back to the UK for legal reasons. All this was very different from the values I had learned as a child: security, permanence, house ownership. Perhaps the freedom of life as an expat could be enticing? (This, by the way, was pre-Brexit.) What is this word 'home' really about, and how important is it? And could I enjoy life as an expat? Why own a house when renting could be much more flexible? Did I want to commit myself deeply to one place when life as an expat seemed so interesting and exciting? These very important fundamental questions stayed with me, and I found some answers later.

It was tough to realise that Gozo was not a place for Rosie the aspiring cellist, but this created the opportunity to address another uncomfortable question: just how big a part of me is my cello, and what might life be like without it? Is the cello a help or a hindrance? Is my love of the cello holding me back from other experiences? In this way, my Gozo experience made me question another fundamental self-belief. The broader suggestion, that I could question some of my fundamental beliefs, remained in the back of my mind until I was ready to grasp this wide-ranging and very challenging opportunity.

Though my love affair with Gozo fizzled out, it laid some important groundwork for my journey and helped me to recognise opportunities. Specifically, my time on Gozo taught me to be open to whatever learning is in store, including what I learn about myself. I appreciated the new friends I made, but I realised it was important to be selective. Circumstances forced me to acknowledge and question some of my preconceptions, and doing this helped me in my future planning. I also learned to accept reality, however harsh. (In this case, that Gozo was not a long-term prospect for me.) Despite this realisation, I gave to, and took from, Gozo what I could, enjoyed a lot of fun and learned a huge amount. I stored many happy memories and came away with important questions to which I hoped to return.

Being ill in December 2015 had had some very beneficial effects! Not least, it had led me to identify some important questions, and to be open to different ways forward.

INSPIRATION THROUGH CONVERSATION

Over the next two years, as it became clearer that Gozo would not be a long-term solution, I had many other random thoughts. I continued my semi-retired life in Lancaster, but the seeds of change had been sown.

I spent a lot of time with my beloved cello, which, in a sense, had taken over my life. More about that later. Alongside this overriding passion, life was quite busy. I kept myself reasonably fit by walking in the beautiful countryside that surrounds Lancaster (including the Lake District), cycling on fine days, beating myself up for enjoying my food too much, and occasionally tackling my overwhelming garden. I exercised the grey cells with my wonderful book group and in two philosophy groups, while continuing to work part-time as a psychotherapist. Because of frequent get-togethers with local friends, Lancaster's wide-ranging cultural events, and occasional contact with my cousins near Warrington, my social life was lively. Strangely (was I on the edge of madness?), I also tried very hard to move to Manchester – the big city where I had a few friends and which offered endless cultural opportunities and a friendly choir I could join. My Manchester friend, Helen, had given me lots of support with this. I changed my mind the day my feet ached after plodding the streets, looking at undesirable, overpriced houses under a grey sky. I caught a slow tram which dragged me across urban wasteland to Piccadilly Station. As I walked home from Lancaster Station, the local orchard was flamboyant with burgeoning blossom, and the familiar-faced dogwalkers smiled. Somehow I came to my senses. (And Helen has now moved to Lancaster!)

But underneath the persistent rhythm of day-to-day life, I continually returned to my question: 'What next?' I found some possible answers through listening openly to friends and acquaintances, then by taking time to ponder on comments which particularly interested me. Several conversations, unplanned and serendipitous, proved crucial. None of these conversations was specifically about me or my issues, and all of them happened during informal social chat. I didn't realise, at the time, how significant people's spontaneous remarks can be. Yet each one caused me to reflect deeply afterwards and moved my thinking forward in ways I couldn't have predicted.

Inspiration over a drink

One of these conversations arose in Gozo while I was considering spending more time there. My friend Jill introduced me to Brenda at the bar during a gig. Brenda is an expat, originally from Sussex. I asked her how she enjoyed life on Gozo. She replied, 'Well, I'm happy here as long as I can get away four times a year.' How important that reply of hers turned out to be! Mulling it over afterwards, I realised it had relevance to me. I had often wondered whether I would stay in Lancaster – a (small-town-sized) city about an hour and a quarter north of Manchester. At the time, I felt I had exhausted much of what Lancaster offered, and I couldn't see it as my lifelong choice. Brenda's comment posed me a new question: What would it be like to live in Lancaster if I could get away for a complete change four times a year? What a difference that made! Living in Lancaster did not mean being imprisoned there. I began to think I could possibly be happy in Lancaster if I made sure I went away frequently enough. I had the beginnings of an important answer.

Inspiration after book group

My book group, which we set up in 2005, provides me with an important social circle, and I have developed fond friendships through it. A bunch of sparky and ageing women, we meet every six weeks and all live in North Lancashire or South Cumbria – so we're happy to travel to each other's homes to talk about a book. It's an enjoyable social event, and there are always drinks and too many biscuits, so we have a lot of opportunities to chat informally. After one session, Geri was telling me how she and her partner, Viv, had recently had a weekend away with family at Machynlleth, where they had visited the Alternative Technology Centre. She spoke with immense warmth, love and enthusiasm about the whole weekend and it touched me deeply. Geri and Viv have some health challenges which can limit their activities, but they still experience great joy. Reflecting on this afterwards, I realised that what they were doing was making the very best of their gifts in the present moment: loving families, the ability to take short holidays and their Buddhist joy in the here and now.

Turning this round, I asked myself, 'So, what are my gifts?' I came up with three answers: good health (long may it last!), complete freedom from family ties and responsibilities, some money in the bank. (My musical gift didn't figure at this point but made its comeback later.) I remembered my belief that to be fulfilled we need to use our gifts, while we can, to the full. It was this thinking that caused me to firm up my ponderings about travel – especially considering that health, when we reach our 60s, cannot be taken for granted. Without dependants I had the gift of personal freedom, and I could afford to pay some fares. My inner voice shouted 'DO IT NOW!' It was at this moment that my decision was made, to travel. Little did Geri know how important and powerful that conversation about her weekend away had been. Everyone's situation differs and determines our options and the choices we make. My thoughts are but one example of how it can help to bring into focus that very important question: 'What are my gifts?'

Inspiration from morose moments

Possibly the most pivotal conversation took place in my Lancaster home, with a friend who was staying for a few days. One evening we were mumbling morosely into our Prosecco when my friend said, 'The thing is, Rosie, I feel so *encumbered*.' The importance of this struck me immediately. 'Encumbered' – what an apt word to use, and how I identified with it! After my friend left, I gave this a lot more thought.

SQUARING UP TO 'ENCUMBRANCE': TODAY'S SECURE ANCHOR, TOMORROW'S BALL AND CHAIN?

It was time for me to stop allowing encumbrances to define me. I defined an encumbrance as anything that was weighing me down, holding me back or limiting my life. Even that definition made me realise I had hit on a huge issue, but I needed to identify my encumbrances, however hard that turned out to be. Oh wow! It was worse than shedding my clothes and posing nude in front of a magnifying mirror – how scary was that? Could this cosy lifestyle of mine, in itself, be, in some way, an encumbrance? This was difficult to contemplate because it meant allowing myself some alien thoughts. So I sat myself down with a huge chocolate brownie (one of my favourite comfort foods), a pen and paper, and as much honesty and courage as I could muster. And I asked myself the following questions:

- What aspects of my life feel burdensome?
- Is there anything that makes me 'lose the will to live'?

- Am I carrying too much?

- What specific aspects of my life lead me to feel 'stuck'?

- To whom do I feel accountable, and is that a good thing?

- Do the people in my life urge me forward or hold me back?

- Do my friends and family boost or undermine my confidence?

- Are there things I believe I'm incapable of – and are those beliefs accurate?

The answers to these questions, to be honest, came out as a jumble of incoherent scrawl. I had to leave the exercise and return to it the next day (this time with a cheese and pickled-walnut sandwich) to give my brain time to recover. Eventually I grouped and organised everything I'd scribbled into the shortest list I could distil. This was the list of my encumbrances:

- **Housequandary**: a nice house but too big, in the wrong place and with an unmanageable garden, and no idea where I want to live

- **Moggiemalady:** my two beautiful cats, who need either feeding at home or accommodation in a cattery whenever I go away, making major travel impossible

- **FOMO (Fear of Missing Out):** my belief that it would be impossible to rebuild my social and musical circles if I went travelling for any length of time

- **Cellomania:** my cello, which absorbs lots of my energy, is cumbersome to carry and doubles the price of air travel because it needs its own seat

- **Oldfogeyness:** my ageing mindset, intolerance, increasing reliance on mindless habits, love of my home comforts and worries about leaving my house unoccupied

- **The 50% club**: my lesbian identity which sometimes narrows my social horizons (many of my social groups are women-only)

It was clear to me that to make the best use of my gifts and to free myself to make the best of any major plans, I needed to shed these encumbrances. This notion of 'shedding' was life-changing. Just how much did I really need to cling to the situations, things and ideas that limited my life? I think this was the most important and powerful question of my whole journey.

DISENCUMBERING: FACING THE GIANT

Of course, there are encumbrances which are very difficult or impossible to shed. In our 60s and 70s many of us have dependants whom we love and for whom we feel responsible. Acknowledging a suppressed longing to break away and do something new can itself bring feelings of guilt – and the guilt can prevent us from considering our options – and even from accepting the word 'encumbrance'. Other ties – such as business interests, health issues, confidence issues – can also hold us back. But please bear with me while I offer, tentatively, some possible approaches. It is worth trying to define your encumbrances without beating yourself up. You might then feel like looking for any aspects of these which you can change. I sometimes find it useful to look at the who, what, where, when, how and why of a specific situation, to bring to light hidden details which could be changed. I also find it important to look critically at my own beliefs and fears, in case any of them are holding me back. If so, can I change them? In the next section, I offer specific examples of beliefs I had to change in order to shed some of my encumbrances.

Making big changes can be difficult, so it is really important to organise some form of support. There might already be people you can immediately trust, not only to respect your deeper thoughts and feelings but also to help you forward rather than hold you back. But sometimes those we are closest to can discourage us from changing because of their own fear of change, so wise choices are needed. The internet offers a wide range of support groups (to be chosen carefully), and self-help books are often linked to supportive websites.

Letting go of anything, and especially encumbrances, can be difficult. I remember Aesop's fable in which a monkey with his hand full of nuts inside a narrow-necked jar was unable to regain his freedom until he let go of the nuts. This was a key lesson for me in my attempts to disencumber. All of the 'encumbrances' I had identified had some benefits, and the disencumbering required me to let go of them all. In each case, I tried to imagine life without that particular encumbrance and its benefits. Slowly I came to realise that imaginings got me nowhere and the only way to disencumber was to take action and let each of them go – along with the risks of doing just that. Of course, that was scary, and I had to deal with the fear. What if I made a mistake? For keen readers, many helpful books exist about fearless decision-making. *Feel the Fear and Do It Anyway* by Susan Jeffers is a must-read. Many books have also been written from a Buddhist perspective about letting go; the writer Jon Kabat-Zinn included a helpful approach in his book *Wherever You Go, There You Are*. An internet search will bring more rich results. At the time, I was too busy to read, and I had already decided that my way forward lay in disencumbering. In fact, I had little to lose by doing so. So I took the plunge.

Whatever your situation, I hope my disencumbering story, offered in greater detail below, might provoke some useful ideas. I saw no alternative but to confront and tackle each of the encumbrances I had identified. Doing so was extremely challenging, but helpful and enlightening.

Housequandary

Although I liked my house and I'd developed it in my own style after Cathy had moved out, I knew it held no future for me. Going away travelling was a good solution to not knowing where I wanted to live; I could put my stuff in storage and delay the decision. But I still could not decide whether to let the house or sell it – and being me, I thoroughly weighed up all the pros and cons but found myself no clearer. The answer to this came to me in a startling way, during my visit to Gozo in January 2018. As usual, I joined the walking group. The expats all had opinions (widely varying) on whether I should sell or let, so I had made no progress with that decision. Perhaps it was the change of diet or environment, but one day I realised I was suffering very uncomfortably from constipation. (Yes, you DO need to know this.) The next morning I awoke with an urgent need to 'go', even before my first cuppa! As I sat enthroned and waited for nature to take its course, my mind returned to that lingering question: sell or let? Then there was a tumultuous event. I had a seismic, and the most satisfying ever, earthquake of a bowel movement. The words 'Let go!' came into my mind – so I did, and boy did it feel good! But wait a minute... What if I let go of the house as well? Let go of the house! And that actually felt like the right thing to do. That wasn't the final decision – after flushing the toilet three times, I took a cup of tea back to bed and contemplated what had just happened. After a few days, the decision became final. This must have been the archetypal outcome of that very sound piece of advice: 'Trust your gut!'

I had worked out a notional timescale for my travel, which was to be a round-the-world trip. I wanted to be free of the hassle of a house sale well before my departure, so I decided to rent for six months before leaving. Luckily my plans worked out and my house sold quickly, so by the time I was ready to leave, it was straightforward simply to give notice on the rented house, store my stuff and go. I was very glad I'd rented, which simplified my life and helped me avoid the stress of selling a house at a time when other big changes were afoot. Some well-intentioned people commiserated when they learned I'd given up my home, but I was always quite certain it was the right thing for me to do, and a logical step in the overall scheme. I had sold my house, but I was not attached to it emotionally, and by selling it I had shed a major encumbrance.

Moggiemalady

Cleocatra and Sophisticat (Cleo and Sophie) were gorgeous moggie princesses who organised my life (on their terms) and sat on me to keep me in my place. Their presence (in addition to dead birds and half-mangled mice) filled the house for eight years and brought me great joy, revulsion and amusement. Life without them was painful to contemplate, but I slowly came to accept that the kindest solution was to let them go and rehome them before going travelling. This wasn't easy, as they were at least nine years old and most people are looking for younger cats. I was also wary of rehoming them via the internet in case they were used as bait in dog fights. I had no luck with local animal shelters, which were all full – and in any case I wanted to know the person who finally took them. Enter Margaret, my inspirational school music teacher, with whom I was (and am) still in touch. Margaret had helped me to develop my confidence as a musician – a huge gift which has enabled me to try different ways of making music and to do quite well in some. We still meet once or twice a year. Margaret had wanted cats for several years, but her back door wasn't suitable for a cat flap. When I told her my plans, she immediately had a new back door, with a cat flap, fitted. This must have been one of my luckiest moments. In early January 2018, I loaded up the car with Cleo, Sophie and all the cat paraphernalia and took them to Margaret in a Manchester suburb. I was sad to part with them but relieved to have found this perfect solution. Rehoming my cats marked an important stage in my planning and disencumbering, giving me the freedom I needed to travel.

FOMO (Fear of Missing Out)

The idea of leaving behind my close friends and my wider social circle worried me. Life moves on, and there was no guarantee that on my return I'd be able to pick up where I'd left off. What if their lives were to change, leaving no gap for me to fill on my return? What if it were I who couldn't settle back into the Lancaster I found if I returned? Could I cope with the loneliness or a feeling that I no longer belonged here? Regarding music, I realised that my string quartet and my baroque group would need to find another cellist to replace me. Would I be able to make new musical connections on my return? For about two years, these fears had prevented me from seeing a way forward. I was stuck in the negative belief that I could not cope with these challenges – what an encumbrance! How could I sort this one out?

What I did was tell my friends about my fears and share my plans more superficially with people I knew less well. I cannot overstate the importance of the support I received from friends for helping me move forward. They gave me the confidence to follow my intuition and formulate my plans. I believe there are very few people who can plan a life-changing experience without a support network, be it friends, family or even an internet-based group with common interests. That support network needs to be identified and nurtured. I am lucky to be part of a wonderful group of independently minded and supportive women who are, effectively, my surrogate family.

My friends' reactions were heartwarming. They were already up to date with my current plans (which had somehow become a major conversation topic – they were very patient and actually very interested), and had offered me a healthy balance of encouragement and concern for my safety and well-being. Their responses to my fears were honest but reassuring; there could be no promises about the future, but the love and goodwill they expressed gave me faith in our friendships. Things might indeed be different on my return, but my friends had no plans to move away, so they'd almost certainly still be there. Cathy reminded me several times that, if need be, for whatever reason, I could simply return to Lancaster and stay with her until I sorted things out. What kindness and what foresight – as I was later to discover!

My book group and walking friends knew more broadly about my plans and were full of encouragement and sensible advice. But one or two conversations convinced me that some of them actively cared about my way forward and wanted to offer any support they could. With such a wealth of goodwill, I managed to overcome my fears. What I distilled was fairly simple: my friends were there for me. In the unlikely event that I lost any friends by going away, it might be because that friendship was nearing its end. In any case, things sometimes change and I would need to adapt.

My musical contacts were more straightforward to manage. My baroque group decided that as long as they had a keyboard player (who provided a bass line anyway) they could manage without a cello for a year and I could join them again on my return. Phew! That was easier than I'd expected, and I was grateful for their flexibility. My string quartet was equally matter-of-fact: we need a cellist, so we'll have to replace you and there's no guarantee you'll be able to rejoin. Hmm, not so good yet utterly reasonable. This was harder to accept, but there was no alternative, so I left the group and wished them well, and they found another cellist. That felt like a loss, but my excitement about other things helped me get over it.

So, in shedding the encumbering fears I had about losing my friendships and social and musical connections, I had made some discoveries: friendships and social connections can be deeper and more reassuring than first expected; connections based around music (or any other activities) might change, but these changes are more about practicalities and aren't personal; if I lose out, there might even be aspects I'm glad to be without. These discoveries enabled me to go away with an optimistic faith in my existing friendships and connections, combined with the acceptance that some things could change – maybe for worse or, more excitingly, for better! I decided to take the risk.

Cellomania

So now to the cello, which changed my life – I kid you not. I have always been a musician and have a chequered history, dipping in and out of different types of music, trying several instruments and various forms of singing. But in 2012 my musical life was empty – which, for a musician, can be frustrating. Turning 60 had focused me on the idea of a bucket list. I had often wondered about playing the cello, and on the day I heard Dvořák's cello concerto performed live, I resolved to make this happen. Within two weeks I had bought a reasonable student cello from a local musician – so I had a new retirement project. To say I was enthusiastic about the cello was an understatement. (I have been described as someone who doesn't do things by halves.) I remember saying, shortly after getting started, 'I don't need a partner now I've found the cello!' (After Cathy and I had split up, I spent a few romantic, challenging and fascinating years seeking a new partner through online introductions; although I made some lasting friendships, I remain happily single.)

In addition to my cello lessons, I often attended residential workshops further afield, to improve my playing and gain experience in small groups. Several times I even bought my cello an airline seat – too risky to put it in the hold – so it could accompany me to Gozo. My baroque buddy, Jude, had invited me to play in an ensemble in Lancaster, which motivated me to practise and really was a lot of fun. This led me to a major search for a baroque-style cello and countless visits to Bob, my very helpful luthier in Manchester. So besotted was I with the cello that I had to find out how it produced such a beautiful sound – so I found a very cheap one to take to bits. I paid £35 for it, the only problem being that the front had come unglued. This started me on another absorbing activity. Using information from the internet and having lots of chats with luthier Bob, I started to 'do up' very cheap cellos and sell them on to beginners. It was a fascinating time during which I learned a phenomenal amount, but the momentum eventually petered out.

Perhaps just as well – my watchful friends finally voiced their concern when my box room contained five cellos, all in need of attention. I managed to bring them all up to a playable standard eventually, and after selling them, I decided to concentrate on playing.

So I hope you can understand how hard it was for me to contemplate life without a cello. Over about five years, it had become not just an interest but a major part of my identity, and I just could *not* see myself separated from it. Yet it would have been too difficult to travel with such a bulky item in addition to a large holdall and small rucksack – not to mention the expense. The decision would be a wrench, so I had to find a different way of looking at it. Standing back, I acknowledged that just a few years previously the cello had not been a part of my life, and although there had been a 'musical vacuum', I had found enjoyment in other things, especially walking and cycling. I did it then, so what if I could do it now? I also began to ask myself whether feeling so dependent on the cello was perhaps bordering on unhealthy, especially as, if I was honest with myself, the cello didn't fill that gap completely. Then came a depressing and perhaps cruel thought: what if the cello was just a distraction from life's deeper questions? Ouch! But it soon became clear to me that 'what if?' questions could not be answered from the comfort of my living room. I would only discover the answers by getting up and trying things out. If the results were hard to take, so be it... Had I really just said that? Well, I really had no choice. So my two cellos were consigned to be put in storage along with the rest of my stuff. Wowwhee – what a disencumbrance!

Oldfogeyness and Stagnata

During my 60s, love of my home comforts and increasing unease about leaving the house unoccupied worked together to undermine my confidence. It was getting easier and easier to stick with daily habits, relax on a sofa with my cats and feel secure behind locked doors. *Coronation Street* again – exciting! By habits, I mean, for example, waking up in my own bed, having a daily hot shower in a familiar bathroom, putting on the same type of comfortable clothes each day and preparing my usual food in a familiar kitchen. The fear of something going wrong at home if I went away was also beginning to bother me, along with the effort needed to prepare the house for my absence. Avoiding burst pipes in the winter became quite a worry, as did the threat of a break-in.

The part of me that was responsible for this reliance on habit I will call Stagnata. Her favourite colour is beige. She loves an easy, ritualised, boring life with little challenge or variation, and wants to feel comfortable. This developing, unhelpful state of mind reminded me of my loving and well-intentioned dad, who, as he aged, made Stagnata his best friend. He became reluctant to break his routine or visit new places, and seemed fearful of the unknown. He became so preoccupied with security that he ensured my parents' home was like Fort Knox. It was an unhappy moment when, recognising that I was becoming rather fond of Stagnata myself, I realised I might so easily follow his example. So I resolved to do something different, and to break away from Stagnata. At least selling the house would stop me worrying about leaving it unattended.

Banishing Stagnata meant deliberately doing some things differently, so I tried this before going away. I started small: making my morning cuppa with proper tea leaves, sleeping in my spare bed sometimes, washing my body parts in a different order, putting different ingredients in my salad, washing up my breakfast stuff immediately. All these actions took me off autopilot and made me think about what I was doing. Sometimes

Stagnata made me lazy, so when I felt up to it, I tried giving myself some easy challenges: walk into town even if it was raining, refuse a chocolate biscuit, go for a slightly longer bike ride, learn that cello piece I'd been putting off. Not only did I feel virtuous if I succeeded with these challenges, I began to move away from taking the easiest option. As a fledgling Grumpy Old Woman, I like quiet cafés without loud and aggressive music, get on the train as quickly as possible to have a chance of a seat, and hate overcooked cabbage. These foibles would not be helpful while travelling, so I had to expand my comfort zone – which meant abandoning old habits. So I occasionally chose a café with loud music and let the rhythm displace my thoughts. I decided it didn't matter if I had to stand on the train, and in any case that would do me good. I allowed overcooked cabbage to pass my lips occasionally – and survived.

Once I was travelling, I had no choice but to make the best of each situation, and Stagnata could not help in new circumstances. Situations, for example, in hostel bathrooms and kitchens...

Can I get in the shower without slipping?

Ouch, that's hot!

Damn – I've left my shower gel in my toilet bag.

Hmm – don't fancy using any of these mugs.

Where on earth are the teabags?

Fwoahhh, this milk stinks!

These irritations arose in new situations where I had to adapt – and things take longer without Stagnata. So I began to accept that I could not be on autopilot. Slow down, approach each situation as a total newcomer, consider each step. Check beforehand whether shower gel is provided. Find something to hold on to when getting in the shower. Test the water temperature first. Wash my chosen mug thoroughly. Take more time to find the teabags. Check the use-by dates before opening any milk. While these more deliberate approaches didn't solve the problem entirely, they certainly made life easier, and I began to appreciate life without Stagnata.

To be fair, habitual behaviour is sometimes helpful. If I need to turn my mind to an important decision or if I get excited by a new idea, it helps if I allow Stagnata to take over some of the more routine events. She will make sure I have my breakfast, so my mind can be free for more important matters. I also realised that, without Stagnata, life can become tiring. Doing things differently uses up mental energy which might be needed for other things. So I decided to allow Stagnata her voice occasionally.

Hello, Stagnata! Make me a cup of tea, please, so I can have a think about planning my trip. And Stagnata, please decide what I will wear today...

One comforting habit I decided to allow myself was to continue to wear the same style of clothes. I like warm leggings, walking shoes and fleeces, which is just who I am, so those things stayed. Jettisoning some of my habitual thoughts and behaviour, however, was an important – if more gradual – means of disencumbering, which helped me to open my mind to new situations, an essential mindset for travelling. If you want to think more about how habits can work with or against you, try *Atomic Habits* by James Clear.

The 50% Club

I grew up conforming to heterosexual norms and, as society expected, married a man. Later, finally accepting that I was strongly attracted to one particular woman, I acknowledged that since my teens I had been quashing such feelings to keep my parents happy and for the sake of 'respectability'. That constant itch to be true to myself was now out of its box and running rampant. The physical aspect of my heterosexual marriage was acceptable but produced no children – which for me was never a big issue. But I was unhappy with other aspects of the relationship and could see no way of improving it. For too many years, though I wanted to make the big change, I lacked the courage to do it and resigned myself to life as it was. I was 45 when my husband found someone else and set me free. Very soon afterwards, discovering my lesbian identity felt like coming home. I have enjoyed life as a lesbian ever since.

Being lesbian naturally led me to seek out social contacts exclusively with women. Working throughout the 1980s in education in Inner London, I had developed feminist views and an intolerance of some 'male' behaviour. So I was happy to spend my social time with women, most of whom held similar (or stronger) feminist views. At first I needed this style of social life, as it helped to reinforce the new sense of self I had adopted. Since coming out, there had been a new 'me' behind these eyes, and she needed nurturing. I enjoyed and appreciated (and still do) the wonderful social life and support networks that exist among lesbian feminists similar in age to me. However, I also realised that Stagnata was very happy to allow me to continue with this social habit, and did not want me to consider its shortcomings.

Ouch! Could my cosy, lesbian circles conceivably be, in some way, limiting? Help! Facing facts, I admitted that socialising exclusively with women meant I was denying myself any enjoyment of male company – not forgetting that men make up around 50% of the population. I admitted that I had sometimes appreciated men's light-hearted banter when I'd come across it on small-group holidays. I admitted that on some all-women holidays, and even in my own social circles, I'd sometimes wanted light relief from intense conversations – including some that I had initiated. I admitted that the sexist behaviour I had experienced in heterosexual relationships had contributed in part to the development of my feminist views, and that some men are enlightened and supportive. I even admitted that I'd been OK with the physical side of my marriage.

So I decided to experiment, while travelling, with shedding the 'lesbian' label and being open to possibilities. This would have been difficult at home because most of my social life was geared to all-women circles, but while away travelling I would not have this limitation. I realised that, after more than twenty years living as a lesbian, it was very unlikely that I would develop a physical relationship with a man, but I decided not to exclude the possibility, however remote. Yes, doing this felt quite brave, but as I was intent on opening up to all life's possibilities, it was necessary.

***

So, there I was in July 2018, feeling as free as I could from the encumbrances which had been holding me back – well, at least the ones I was aware of. The disencumbering took time and a lot of thought – definitely not an overnight achievement. But I eventually felt ready to move ahead with THE GRAND PLAN. It was an exciting time, but I also harboured some apprehension. Having come so far, what if something, unpredictably, went wrong? What if Sod's Law kicked in and I had to abandon the plan? I spent the next fourteen months doing my best to balance this niggling, underlying fear with my excitement and optimism about the way forward.

SECTION 2: MAKING IT HAPPEN

WHIMS + IDEAS = HONESTY!

So – wow – this was real! Over the two years between December 2015 and the end of 2017, my complicated ponderings had led me to decide on a major project with the possibility of huge life changes. By July 2018, my house was sold and I was about to embark on some kind of long journey, but I still had only a few ideas and no definite plan – and time was passing. Here are the thoughts I started with:

- **Be open to settling somewhere completely new.** I'd sold my house and was intending to sell my car and store everything else, so, without dependants, I could choose to live anywhere – literally. I wanted to travel with a completely open mind that would allow me to create a new life anywhere I chose, if that felt right. I didn't want any opportunity to pass me by.

- **Focus on the people I will meet.** I believe it is local people who bring a place to life and give it character, so when I wasn't on the 'tourist trail', I wanted to focus on meeting living people rather than photographing statues, being a traveller rather than a tourist. I believed that I would learn more through conversation than I would through reading and absorbing information.

- **Be open to whatever emotions arise as a result of my experience, including any negative ones.** I would embrace the amazement, the disappointment, the fear, the sadness. This would be an important way of finding out what really mattered to me.

- **Visit family in Australia.** Two family members went to Australia as 'Ten Pound Poms' two generations ago. I wanted to meet my cousins there for the first time.

- **Catch up with my friend Janine who had emigrated to Australia.** She had been, potentially, more than a friend, and the feelings were mutual. We both struggled when her long-established plans finally caused her to leave the UK. Despite complications, I had to find out what was possible for us. I had always tried to make careful, considered decisions about relationships, but that hadn't worked (in my marriage, for example), so this time I wanted to follow my heart.

- **Experience Uluru.** I had heard about Uluru and its importance to the Aboriginal people. I wanted to experience its magic and gain some understanding of Aboriginal philosophy, their lifestyles and the issues they faced.

- **Be stunned by New Zealand.** I had heard about the beauty of New Zealand and how many Brits felt 'at home' there when they visited, so I wanted to see it for myself and try it out.

- **Join a baroque music workshop on a remote Canadian island.** I had discovered it by chance while surfing the net – a one-week event entitled Denman Baroque. This intrigued me, and I'd held it at the back of my mind for several years.

- **Cross the South Pacific.** Naïve though I was, the musical *South Pacific* had filled me with romantic notions of Tahiti. I wanted to experience it, to see and hear musicians and dancers wearing grass skirts, and to go to remote places.

- **See the Grand Canyon and El Capitan.** Bucket-list stuff. After seeing images of the Grand Canyon, I wanted to experience and be stunned by its vastness. I was captivated by El Capitan in Yosemite National Park after seeing documentaries about how people managed to climb it.

- **Go to Mexico.** I had formed impressions of Mexico as a colourful country with sombreros and a Latin feel, so was attracted to it.

- ***Experience India and its 'otherness'.*** I wanted to challenge myself with the huge differences I had observed between life in India and in the UK. (Ultimately, I realised that this would need more time than I had available, so I decided to save India for another time.)

- ***Keep myself safe.***

These ideas became the foundations of my plan and enabled me to list the countries I would include in the trip. Yes, many of my thoughts arose from flights of fancy. In truth, that didn't matter. The underlying purpose of the whole venture was to connect with new people, experimenting with who I was and who I might become. Those discoveries could happen any time, anywhere. At this planning stage, I took note of every whim, no holds barred.

I was planning to travel, but you might have different ideas and aspirations. Whatever you are planning, this process of identifying all your whims – at least as a starting point – could prove indispensable.

COMMITMENT WITH FLEXIBILITY

My list of ideas led me to consider a round-the-world trip. 'Down Under' featured large in the itinerary, and being aware of the extreme temperatures in parts of Australia, I wanted to be there when the climate was tolerable. So Australia had to happen in their autumn, winter or spring. Another fixed point was May 2019, when I wanted to spend a week on Denman Island, Western Canada, to join rehearsals for a staged production of Purcell's *The Fairy-Queen*. Committing to Denman caused me to plan to travel westward in April 2019. Going on to parts of the USA and Mexico, then crossing the Pacific, it should be possible to arrive in Australia in September 2019, their spring.

I had to be flexible about my final plan. Further information caused me to change my mind about Mexico. My timescale would take me to Mexico during their hurricane season, and I came across warnings about the safety of tourists there. Being a solo female traveller, these warnings dented my confidence, so I decided to find an alternative. I knew that Cathy, who loves to speak Spanish, wanted to visit South America, so we decided to spend the month of July together in Peru, to include a three-week, full-on, small-group tour. This would allow me the month of August to cross the Pacific before reaching Australia. Another tick in the box.

By September 2018, I was firmly committed to my plan but still had no idea how to cross the Pacific. I was aware of the need to start booking flights but had little idea of what was possible. How could I cross the Pacific, from Peru to Australia via Tahiti – and what other stops were possible on the way? And then, how could I predict which countries would bring the greatest rewards, when I didn't have a crystal ball or the slightest idea how to use one? It was the availability of flights that finally determined my plan, and I bought a round-the-world plane ticket. I would leave in April 2019 and plan to return to the UK in April 2020. My intended route was Canada to the US to Peru to Easter Island to French Polynesia to the Cook Islands to Australia to New Zealand, then back to Australia, and then Thailand before returning to the UK. 'Aye, aye!' I hear you say, along with, 'What about Covid?' Well, in September 2018, Covid was unheard of, so I went ahead in blissful ignorance. I also booked some small-group trips in advance, to ensure that I had in-depth experiences of the places that mattered to me.

KINDNESS AND COMPANY, THROUGH SERVAS

I was worried that travelling solo for a year could be a lonely experience. Hotel rooms, though often comfortable, are usually more expensive than hostels and can give a sense of isolation. It's sometimes easier to meet people in hostel kitchens and common rooms, but I wasn't confident that I'd have much in common with 20-somethings with a different first language. Now come on, Rosie, what was all that about challenging an ageing mindset? Well, OK, I would always be open to a chat. But I also wanted to be realistic. I felt that after a day on the road I might be too tired to initiate conversation in a different language with a much younger person. This fear of loneliness occupied my mind for quite a while.

I think it was Helen who told me about Servas, because she has friends who are members. Servas is a surprisingly little-known organisation whose mission is to promote world peace and international understanding. It was set up in 1949 in Denmark. Members of Servas offer, typically, two nights' accommodation and meals to traveller members, and they will often show guests round their local area or include them in their day-to-day activities. Travellers usually offer accommodation themselves when at home. Membership is inexpensive but requires form-filling and a face-to-face chat, which constitutes a mild vetting process. Members then post a profile on the Servas website, both as hosts and as prospective guests. For a solo woman traveller, Servas therefore offers a reasonably safe means of finding accommodation and meeting local people. So, I joined.

Looking through the international directory, I discovered many members in places where I would need accommodation, so I started by contacting someone on Vancouver Island. On receiving her welcoming reply, I was inspired to try again. By the time I left for Vancouver, I had arrangements to stay with several Servas members in Canada. More on that later. For now, I will just say that Servas gave me confidence that I could safely travel solo without feeling lonely and get the feel of a place by meeting real people. My travels would have been much more difficult and lonely without Servas, which became crucial for the success of my journey.

Whatever you are planning, it is worth the effort to research organisations which can offer you support with your venture.

SERENDIPITY, NOT ANONYMITY! OPPORTUNITIES TO CONNECT

Once my route, in broad terms, was decided, I started on the detail. I wanted to maintain my focus on meeting local people, and ideally, I hoped to find introductions via friends. If this didn't work, I would try Servas, and failing that, I would book accommodation I could cancel easily. One thing was certain: I would need to seek opportunities and embrace serendipity. I'd have to be willing to talk to anyone and everyone very openly about my plans, and about my need for ideas, introductions, contacts and accommodation. With any kind of venture, it is helpful to seek out a wide range of contacts who can offer help, useful suggestions and information. This might not be easy for everyone, and it can test our confidence, but I was astonished at the positive responses I received – and the more people I approached, the easier it became.

People's responses were amazingly generous. I was pleasantly surprised that everyone, including folks I didn't know very well, was interested in what I was doing and seemed keen to help if they could. (This was only the beginning of a growing web of kindness and opportunity which cushioned my whole journey, and I seriously questioned whether I truly deserved it.) Before leaving the UK, I received several introductions and very generous offers of accommodation. I cannot overstate how a few serendipitous conversations led me to some truly wonderful connections and experiences. I outline below the various opportunities, coincidences and kindnesses that made such an impact on my journey.

Opportunity 1: I had enjoyed meeting Dinah, from Vancouver, on a previous walking holiday, but we had lost touch. Then after another local friend met her coincidentally on a different holiday, Dinah needed accommodation in Lancaster, and through this connection came to stay with me briefly. As a result, she kindly invited me to stay in her Vancouver apartment before and after my trip to Denman Island. This provided a wonderful start to my travels, and she even met me at the airport when I landed in Vancouver. Dinah also introduced me to her friend Chrissy, who was planning to visit one of the local islands at the same time as me. We kept in touch and spent an enjoyable evening on Gabriola, walking the coastline and going to a dance.

Dinah and I then re-established ourselves as travelling companions when she decided to join me on my Grand Canyon trip.

Opportunity 2: Rose, a Lancaster counselling colleague who had lived in Vancouver, introduced me to four wonderful people who were pleased to show me round and spend time with me. My time with each of them was enriching in different ways. Henry and Samuel are proud First Nation people who gave me stark insight into their difficulties living in Vancouver. Rose also introduced me to Laura, whom I met for a meal in a restaurant, and her Kurdish-Iranian friend Ava, who invited me to her home and offered me wonderful company, kindness and hospitality.

Opportunity 3: Celia and Sharon, friends who then lived locally, arranged an invaluable introduction. When I told them about my plan to visit New Mexico (next best thing to Mexico in the US), they mentioned their friend Kerry from Albuquerque. Kerry just happened to be in the UK, attending a Buddhist festival not far from Lancaster, and just happened to be planning a trip to Lancaster immediately afterwards. So we arranged to meet in a café. Straight away, Kerry invited me to stay with her in

Albuquerque, which I did for a total of nine days. While I was there, I went to various Buddhist events with her, met her friends, and she organised a camping trip to Chaco Canyon, a surreal, remote desert location in the (truly) Wild West – one of the highlights of my whole trip.

Opportunity 4: Another friend, Dorothy, has a brother, Andrew, who was then living in Lima, and she introduced us. Andrew, whom Cathy and I met on our second day in Peru, was a brilliant host. He took us on a walking tour of Lima, which included lunch at a restaurant offering ceviche, a (strong-tasting!) national dish of raw fish, raw onions and sweetcorn. At the end of my time in Peru, after Cathy had returned to the UK, Andrew and I met several times to visit more sights, and he gave me his spare ticket to a very unusual ocarina recital given by a Japanese visitor to Lima. Lima was not my favourite city, so I greatly appreciated Andrew's company. He lifted my spirits during my last few days in Peru.

Opportunity 5: I had already briefly met Anita, from the Australian Blue Mountains, when she was staying with another friend in Lancaster. At that time, I had nothing more than a vague thought of going to Australia, but I had mentioned it. Anita invited me, emphatically, to get in touch if I did plan a trip, as she wanted to show me the country of which she was, and is, so very proud. Anita became a cornerstone of my Australian experience. She met me when I landed in Sydney and organised accommodation for us with her friends. We spent three very full and fascinating days exploring Sydney and its surroundings. Arriving in Australia felt like a major milestone in my travels. Anita's warm welcome and good company were especially important to me at a time when I would not have wanted to be alone. Later in the trip, Anita twice invited me to stay with her in the Blue Mountains, where she included me in all her activities and introduced me to friends. She took me on a road trip to visit her brother on his farm in the outback, and her sister, Kath. In New South Wales, I witnessed firsthand the damage caused by drought and the devastating effects on farming. I could say much, much more about all the kindness Anita showed me, but I hope this is enough to show how important that original, brief meeting in Lancaster turned out to be.

Opportunity 6: Through a local walking group, I got to know Jean, who introduced me to her Melbourne friend, Sue. After two WhatsApp video calls, Sue and I decided to meet first in Tasmania. But for Sue, I would never have experienced Maria Island, a nature reserve where we stayed for two nights in a bunkhouse. It was a very special place where I was lucky enough to see a Tasmanian devil. I then stayed in Melbourne with Sue, briefly, before leaving for New Zealand, and on my return to Australia I stayed with her again for longer. She welcomed me into her world and introduced me to her friends, and as I became increasingly familiar with Melbourne, I began to ask myself whether it might be a good place to live.

Opportunity 7: My friend Helen, from Kendal (not to be confused with Helen from Manchester), whom I knew through the book group, had spent time in New Zealand. She put me in touch with her friends Gwenda and Dottie, who live near Tauranga. Though Gwenda was away when I passed through, I spent several very enjoyable days with Dottie at a time when I needed to recuperate from a chest infection. We took things gently and I felt pampered.

Opportunity 8: A few months before I left Lancaster, I went on a residential music course. During convivial meals around large tables I was always glad to talk about my travel plans. One lunchtime, Elaine, my bass-playing friend from Kent, suddenly went quiet and started scribbling on bits of paper. A few minutes later she presented me with contact details of several people in New Zealand, where her daughter lives and where she herself had travelled a few years previously. I followed these up. Some people's circumstances had changed, but thanks to Elaine, I experienced two very warm and enjoyable events. Aart, a school music teacher, invited me to his home in Dunedin, where he lent me a cello. I (by that time disastrously out of practice) had a great time stumbling my way through some Vivaldi, with him on keyboard. In Nelson, I spent an indulgent evening with Trish, Elaine's daughter, who told me about her busy life and her involvement in local theatre and the arts. All this because of a chance conversation over lunch!

I hope this illustrates how crucial it was to talk about my plans and to be open to opportunities. Doing so led to a rich variety of enjoyable experiences in the company of people who had at first been strangers. The people I met showed me huge and wide-ranging generosity and helped me to bridge the gaps between more isolated times, so they were all invaluable for the success of my travels. I learned so much more through them than I could ever have gleaned from books or the internet, and I still feel the warmth of their kindness. Talking and listening brought huge rewards – and can help with any kind of venture.

THE BATTLE OF THE BULGE

I'd always had a flabby tummy but otherwise considered myself fit for my age. I cycled, walked and was generally active. However, during a health check in 2018, the zealous nurse (who was on a serious mission!) measured my belly and told me I was in danger of diabetes. Surprise, surprise: when my test results came through, my blood sugar was at 6.0 mmol/L – which she told me was the bottom end of prediabetic. OMG! What would it do to my travel insurance premium, and the risks of travelling, if I were diagnosed as diabetic? The nurse prescribed me twelve sessions at the local gym and a rigorous study course on diabetes, and advised me to lose weight. I skipped the course but did the gym sessions, ate fewer calories and gave up alcohol. I won't deny the additional incentive of, perhaps, losing some flab to look more attractive – vanity has its blessings. And more seriously, I didn't fancy being ill somewhere remote like the Cook Islands.

The difference at the end of the gym sessions, combined with seriously reducing the carbohydrates in my diet, was astonishing. After a period which included Christmas (when the odd drink or six did grace my throat), I had lost about a stone and my blood pressure was lower than average for my age. I felt healthier, lighter and more energetic. But interestingly, my blood sugar had only fallen to 5.9 mmol/L. All that effort to very small effect! What the gym sessions did prove to me was the importance of more strenuous and regular exercise. So I kept up the gym and was careful with what I ate and drank right up to the time of my departure. The new look required new clothes, so I (unusually for me) developed great delight in buying yet more bargain-price, comfortable gear. I also resolved never to put the weight back on... Hmmm...

Leaving for my travels in a slimmer body was good for my confidence, and an improvement in my mental clarity helped me stay focused when I needed to plan, book hotels and use the internet. I had little fear of being seriously ill, which gave me the courage I needed in remote places. So I am glad I 'took myself in hand' to maximise my chances of success – though it would have been so easy to ignore the nurse's advice.

DEFEATING THE DREADED PACKING!

I hate packing. Too many lists, too much running up and down stairs for all those small but essential items, too exhausting – and then there's always something crucial I've forgotten (Swiss Army knife, nail file, lip salve, insect repellent – that kind of thing). So I kept delaying in the hope that I would wake up one morning and find everything packed. No such luck! The question remained: how would I pack for a year away, moving through different climate zones, and keep it manageable?

But before packing for my travels I had to pack up my home – twice. The first time was when I moved into a smaller, rented house. The second time was when I put everything into storage. These events gave me great opportunities to downsize. It was a true disencumbering. I hit my garage with a fury before selling my house; it hadn't been sorted since I moved in. Things I had forgotten existed (apart from the spiders) were given away or sold using Freegle, Facebook or our local Swapshop. My house buyers bought some of my furniture. Books I hadn't opened for years went to Oxfam, along with many CDs and piles of sheet music. I decimated my wardrobe, which included things I had last worn years before while working in London. I kept only the furniture I liked, or which I knew would be useful in the rented house. A young couple dismantled my king-size bed and took it, along with every piece of king-size bedding I owned. Shedding these extraneous possessions was sheer therapy, in very practical terms. Life suddenly felt simpler. Moving a vastly reduced set of possessions into my rented accommodation was easier than I had expected. Transferring my stuff into storage, from the rented house, was a breeze. I disposed of a few more things which were neither use nor ornament, and the removal firm took the rest. And yes, this included my two push-bikes and two cellos. I was left with just the items I would need on my travels. It's hard to describe the sense of freedom I felt on the day this happened. But my life felt as if it had been scoured squeaky-clean.

My travels would include some hiking, so I either had to carry everything with me permanently (fifty-litre rucksack?) or leave most of my stuff in a safe place and carry a daysack. Did I really consider fifty litres? For a whole year away in various climates? What planet was I living on? My whole life would need to fit into my luggage. I wanted to feel clean, but I wasn't prepared to wash my underwear every night or sacrifice some comforts to achieve this, so I needed more capacity. I already had a strong eighty-litre holdall with wheels, so I decided to pack my world into this, keeping it as lightweight as possible, and carry a daysack for my immediate needs. Strictly speaking, even this combination didn't give me enough space, and at around thirty pounds, it was as heavy as I could comfortably handle. Fortunately, Cathy was happy to receive parcels from me when I bought new things and needed to offload others. Several times, in places where I trusted the postal service, I made a point of going through my stuff and sending a parcel to Lancaster. This was always satisfying.

There is no universal packing list, but here are a few decisions I made:

- I needed reading material, a comfortable screen for writing, and my mobile phone. Books would be too heavy. I took my mobile and the lightest ten-inch tablet I could find so I could read ebooks and write my blog. It helped that my phone and tablet were the same make so that they would sync, and this combination worked well for all my IT needs.

- I wanted to carry a musical instrument, so I allowed myself a harmonica (waste of space – I never learned to play it) and a plastic (damage-proof) recorder. I sent both of these back to the UK quite early. Making noise in hotels or other people's homes didn't feel right, and somehow, in these circumstances, I lacked motivation.

- I travelled in my hiking boots, to leave more space in my luggage. My only other footwear consisted of a pair of walking sandals and some light trainers, which were enough for my whole time away, although I would have liked some lightweight, waterproof shoes.

- To survive in different climates, I took light clothes which could be layered. Merino T-shirts were useful, as they could be used as vests. I succumbed to the idea of washing underwear regularly so carried only four pairs of briefs. My only coat was a lightweight, breathable waterproof. Zip-off trousers gave me flexibility for the lower half. My only towel was a lightweight one for travel. All of these decisions served me well to keep the weight down.

- I used a TSA padlock on my holdall so that customs officers would be able to search my bag without damaging it (not that I ever thought my bag had been searched), and a bright red luggage strap so I could easily recognise my bag at reclaim – easy additions that minimized travel stress.

- I left room for some basic food, plastic cutlery, an airtight plastic box and a water bottle. I used all of these when I had no access to shops, cafés or clean water.

- My health needs included a small first-aid kit, insect repellent, sunscreen, lip salve, anti-inflammatories, a knee support, walking poles and zinc tape to prevent blisters. I didn't compromise and was glad of all these items, for quality of life.

- I hate arriving exhausted and having to rummage endlessly to find something, so I sorted my stuff into differently coloured dry-sacks: tops, bottoms, smalls, swimmies, bits'n'pieces, etc., and I labelled each bag with black felt-tip. I still use these dry-sacks when I travel – and I can usually dig out the required item quickly.

- I took a money belt for the times when I needed to be careful in public places. This gave me an added sense of safety.

- Despite all this careful planning, I managed to make one mistake twice: I forgot to stow my penknife in my hold luggage. Of course, airport security confiscated it. I bought a replacement, then let the same thing happen again – and I gave myself a good slap!

Overall, I was glad of the decisions and compromises I made, as I was able to carry my essentials in luggage I could handle. It was important to be realistic and pragmatic. With hindsight, I realise it was very important to build in a fail-safe option – in that I could send parcels back to Cathy's home in Lancaster if I needed to offload. It was important to analyse the potential weak spots in my plan and to have a plan B.

Going away for a year with just my two bags resonated with the idea of disencumbering. I had shed not only encumbering attitudes and responsibilities but also a huge number of possessions. It was liberating to see my world packed up and ready to go, with only what I needed and no unnecessary or unwanted burdens.

ORGANISATION: THE PRICE OF SANITY

As April 2019 approached, I had an ever-increasing fear that something might go wrong and prevent me from travelling, so the excitement of my final preparations (though they were going according to plan) was paralleled by a sense of living on the edge. I couldn't allow myself total certainty, and cordoned off a part of myself which was prepared for the worst! It was a very strange time.

I did manage, however, to keep myself busy with the practical arrangements. I allowed my Virgoan attention to detail to wax unfettered, and this was the result:

- About six months before I left, I renewed my passport – just in case my return to the UK was delayed beyond the expiry of my old one – and I checked the immunisation requirements and advice for the countries I would visit.
- I needed visas for Canada, the US, Australia and New Zealand. Sorting those out was a large and tedious admin job.

- About three weeks before I left, I sold my car. Garaging it would have been expensive. I didn't know anyone with spare space on their driveway. And after leaving the car for a year – or what if I didn't come back at all? – its value would have depreciated. Local car dealers, as well as the bigger ones, left me utterly depressed. What to do for the best occupied my mind for about three months. But I told everyone I knew that I needed to sell, and finally arranged a personal sale to a couple of friends, which gave them a very good deal and gave me more than I could have made commercially. The reality of my plans began to sink in when I had delivered the car – cleaned, valeted and sparkling – to Kendal and was waiting bereft at Oxenholme Station for a train back to Lancaster. I was carless for the first time in over forty years but glad I had one fewer worry to leave behind.

- I searched for Servas hosts in all the countries I planned to visit, and found no one in any of my Pacific Island destinations. I'd also heard that accommodation could be expensive, especially in Tahiti. So I booked all my Easter Island, French

Polynesia and Cook Islands accommodation before leaving the UK in the hope that early booking would be cheaper. It still cost me – ouch! – loadsamoney, but at least I felt secure that I wouldn't arrive in remote places as a complete stranger with nowhere to stay.

- I moved out of my rented house a week before my departure, put my stuff in storage and forgot about it. Then I went to stay with Cathy. This meant that during my final few days the hard work of packing up my stuff (again!) had already been done, and I could concentrate on goodbyes. All I took to Cathy's were my two travel bags and another bag of 'last days in Lancaster' clothes, which remained at Cathy's when I left. This was now, definitely, beginning to feel real.

- I told my English cousins and people on my Christmas card list what I was doing so no one was left wondering.

- Cathy and I agreed that I could use her address for post. I wanted to keep my UK bank account, so all written correspondence was received there, and I notified the relevant organisations about my change of address.

- I didn't want to start my journey without friends on the station platform to wave me off – fears of a lonely goodbye! There was no guarantee when, or if, I would see them again, and I knew I needed people there when my train pulled out of Lancaster Station. Luckily a suitable train left in the afternoon, so I organised lunch in a nearby pub and invited my closest friends and others who had helped me with the planning. This was a good move.

- I arranged to meet my second cousin Margaret, for lunch before leaving Heathrow – another means of reminding myself that I was not alone in the world and a good way to touch base with one of my few family members.

- I investigated how to use my mobile phone abroad and decided to buy a local SIM in each country. This was in 2019.

- I set up a blog to update friends and to have a record of my experiences. This worked well enough for me as a writer, but I unfortunately neglected to check how easy it would be for readers to access and comment on my blog. I chose the wrong platform, which most people found either unreliable or very difficult to use. As a result, a few stalwart friends responded to my blog posts throughout, but many people gave up in frustration.

- I agreed to give Cathy details of where I would be staying whenever I was not with friends, family or Servas hosts. I also promised to check in with her briefly on arriving anywhere. It was helpful to both of us, knowing Cathy would be alerted quickly if anything went wrong.

- I took out a year's travel insurance. There are policies which allow you to stay away for a whole year, but you have to shop around and read the small print.

- I opened a credit card account which could work in any currency and offered good exchange rates. A lesson I learned from this experience was to ensure that the credit card company would be willing to log my new mobile number with each change of SIM card. Mine was unable to change from my obsolete UK number (even though it was a card claiming to be designed for travel!), so communication with that company was not straightforward.

Making this final action list (which took shape over a long period and received additions whenever they came to mind) enabled me to move forward with relative peace of mind and a sense that everything was under control. Seeing to all the items I had listed also displaced some of my worries when I feared that something could so easily go wrong.

AMAZINGLY, THE BIG DAY ARRIVES!

There happened to be a meeting of my book group two days before I left. This was extended into a meal with shared food, hosted by Liz in Kendal. I realised quite late that the meal had been organised in honour of my departure. Cathy provided bubbly, and eleven of us enjoyed a large and tasty buffet. Good wishes flowed in abundance, and I had an opportunity to update everyone on my plans. I was touched by the care and support I received from my book-group friends, and was gratified that here were people for whom my plans held significance. It was good to know they were with me in spirit.

When I awoke on Easter Sunday, 21st April 2019, satisfied that I had finally done all I could to prepare for my travels, my main emotion was relief. I wasn't ill and no major disasters had befallen me. All I had to do was pack the final items, have lunch with my friends near the station, and get on a train – and it was a beautiful day!

I had known that the start of my travels would be a very important day for me, and I was glad I had organised a special event to mark this. The time we spent together over lunch was precious. We were a happy group of eleven. I was able to enjoy my final two hours in Lancaster with my close friends and to thank again several others who had introduced me to people I would meet on my travels. I veered from excited to incredulous that this day had arrived according to plan and that the adventure and psychological experiment I had set up were – yes – becoming real. We had time for group photos in the pub garden before my friends walked the short distance to Lancaster Station with me – just to make sure I went! The final photos were taken on platform 4 amid hugs and good wishes (everyone tactfully keeping any worries or sadness unaired). Eventually the train doors closed behind me and the waving hands on Lancaster Station disappeared from sight. Gulp!

I sat down in a daze. Emotionally exhausted, exhilarated, tearful, joyful... This rollercoaster lasted until I fell asleep briefly. Awaking with a jolt and relieved I hadn't missed my stop, I had to work out the final stages of the day's journey. Destination: a budget hotel near Heathrow Airport. It meant a long haul through Reading (Sunday engineering works) followed by a bus ride and a walk, but at least I got the measure of handling my luggage. Fortunately the twenty-minute walk was manageable. I collapsed onto the bed in my hotel room and reflected on my exhaustion. Apart from being physically tired from the practicalities and travelling, I had experienced a range of strong emotions. I was in a state of high excitement at the start of my trip, sad to say goodbye to friends, gratified that they all wished me well, and apprehensive at the enormity of what I was taking on, with my old life behind me and an undefined future. It had been a very big day!

I did eventually get some sleep. The following day, Margaret, my second cousin, picked me up outside the hotel and took me for lunch with her husband Peter – my final meal in the UK. By the time my plane took off, Vancouver-bound, I felt that I'd already come a very long way.

SECTION 3: INTO THE UNKNOWN

So now it was really happening. I had started a journey, both geographical and mental, during which I would see many sights and experience new, exciting and maybe challenging situations. I was open to the possibility that one of my destinations might become a new home, and willing to redefine who I was or might become. My original voluminous travel blog, with photos, charts the whole journey in detail, but that is not my purpose here. Rather, I hope to draw out some important themes which are relevant to the idea of positive ageing, and illustrate them with specific anecdotes and examples. I happened to choose travel for my positive ageing experience. Even if you are on a different kind of journey, I hope some of the things I consider will be helpful and stimulating.

STAYING STRONG

With increasing age, a loss of confidence is common. Sometimes other people's assumptions that we are incapable can influence our own self-beliefs. We are surrounded by younger people who often have a better grasp of modern technology. Well-meant warnings from loved ones can cause us to hesitate before taking on physical tasks. And sometimes, frankly, it's easier just to go along with expectations. This means that making a major change might feel extra difficult, or even impossible, as we get older. I chose, as my main activity, an area in which I already felt confident. Travelling might not be the right decision for everyone. But it is worth considering whether your strong start would be easier to achieve in a familiar activity or in something new and entirely different.

I have always enjoyed travel, and some would view me as a 'seasoned traveller'. I am lucky to have experienced a wide range of holidays – many off the beaten track in small groups, in less-wealthy countries – and a small amount of business travel. So I had already learned the rudiments of international travel, including what can go wrong. I gained most of this experience travelling with someone, which was especially helpful in new or challenging situations: 'Don't forget, we'll need some food for the plane.' 'Where did they say we had to go to get a visa?' 'Are you packing your electric trouser press?' 'Do you think this hotel looks OK?' 'Shall we drink the tap water or buy bottled?' 'Does my bum look big in this?'

Then, having learned the ropes, I started travelling alone, at first for short periods: four days on the long-distance Coast and Castles cycle route, five days on Gozo. It was exciting to join small groups as a solo traveller in countries such as Malawi and South Africa, with every country presenting new situations. But I also gained confidence from things going wrong and having to change plans. Our group missed the plane home from Malawi, so we grudgingly faced the prospect of four extra days in Lilongwe, the capital, with no money left. In the end, our tour leader organised different flights which arrived at a different UK airport twelve hours later than originally scheduled – inconvenient but not life-threatening. Another time my train to Manchester Airport broke down. The suspense of wondering whether I would make it to the plane was intensely stressful. Once I realised I'd completely missed the plane to Malta and been spared a frantic, cello-laden dash through the airport, I could breathe again. I used my phone and credit card to book a flight early the next morning and a hotel near the airport – minimum stress and a new plan. And I could claim on my travel insurance.

Realistically, my confidence as a traveller had developed gradually throughout my life. Without it, my grand plan would have been impossible, so I felt lucky that life events had paved the way. What I learned from these experiences is that most problems, even if they cause irritation and inconvenience, can be solved without undue stress with a flexible attitude and timely use of phone and credit card. This prior experience had been crucial in enabling me to plan my year away with confidence. My policy was to say 'yes' to any apparently safe opportunity and to my experiences in general.

In my view, staying strong depends heavily on prior experience – including mishaps. Learning can provide an informed sense of trust, that problems usually have solutions and need not be catastrophic. This provides peace of mind in relatively new situations. If you need to develop your confidence, consider taking the necessary time to do it in small steps. And if someone can accompany you in the early stages of your learning, you will be able to discuss the next step without feeling alone.

PEOPLE TO APPRECIATE – AND SOME TO AVOID!

If the aim of a major life change is to seek self-fulfilment, most people choose to go it alone. Otherwise the compromises needed when another person is involved can undermine one's own needs. But almost everyone needs some form of day-to-day company. The questions are about how much and what kind.

I knew travelling alone would present me with my own company in large doses. I was brought up as an only child and was accustomed to amusing myself and making my own decisions, so I wasn't too worried about being alone for some of the time. The fact that I was in touch with people via phone, email and WhatsApp also makes me question whether I truly was 'alone'.

On reflection, I experienced widely varying company – and sometimes a lack of it. On arriving in someone's home, I wanted, and made the effort, to communicate fully out of a genuine desire to get to know my host and also to show my appreciation. As a sociable person, I enjoyed this. After time on the road, usually alone, it was always good to relax physically and fall into unpredictable conversation with a new person. Finding common ground added an extra dimension. With Dorothy in San Francisco and with Kaya in Crabbes Creek, both of whom had psychotherapy backgrounds, I could 'speak the same language'. With Kerry in Albuquerque, I could share my experiences with Buddhism. With Hilda and Bridget in Thames, North Island, it was good to acknowledge – often humorously – our shared orientation. I would go to bed 'talked out' and exhausted but hugely enriched.

There were many other evenings when I was with friends, family or a Servas host for a second or third night. These occasions brought me closer to normality because each of us felt more able to relax. While I welcomed the opportunity to wind down, such evenings are less memorable.

Alone but not lonely

The fascination of first-time meetings contrasted starkly with my many (183 in all, I think) nights in booked rooms, often a good distance from evening entertainment, where I was physically alone. Many rooms had a telly, but I had come to appreciate and miss the quality of British drama – and in any case I am no great fan of 'screen time'. My time was entirely my own, which at first felt daunting. It could be difficult to fill six or seven hours alone in a hotel room, so I gradually developed a routine. Yes, Stagnata helped out here with some useful habits:

- I love my food, so of course, it needed organising. When possible I self-catered, especially if the room had a fridge, and finding a local shop became a priority. I lived on salad and combined whatever protein, fresh fruit and veg I could find. This worked well, especially if I was staying more than one night and could buy in quantity. I remember the Bay Village hotel in Cairns, where my room was upgraded free of charge and I enjoyed a very comfortable six-night stay in a one-bedroom apartment. Second choice was to find a café. Failing that I usually carried some food, such as cheese, crackers, nuts, cereal and/ or fruit. I looked forward to my meals, and when time allowed, I revelled in preparing and eating them.

- I always searched online for local evening entertainments, in case there was something appealing and accessible on foot – and if I had the energy after travelling. I could then organise my evening around that. But apart from the occasional cinema visit, this usually drew a blank because cheaper accommodation was almost always a good distance from any major centre, so I was left to my own devices.

- There was almost always a plan for the next day which needed to be finalised. This meant pinning down the detail such as bus times, opening times, walking routes and accommodation arrangements. Much of this I could do online, but if I needed a particular bus stop or meeting place the next morning, I always went out to find it the evening before, to prevent a last-minute panic. I learned this from discovering one day that the walk to the bus stop was going to take me twice as long as I'd expected, and dragging a thirty-three-pound bag over uneven pavements in a desperate hurry was not fun.

- Once I had dealt with the necessities, there was time to relax. I enjoyed checking and replying to my messages and, at the end of a 'chapter' of my travels, writing the next instalment of my blog. Late evenings also gave me an opportunity to read. After that, on rare occasions when I had energy to spare, my mind occasionally wandered into creativity and I dreamed up new ideas or a poem emerged. Others might prefer streaming, computer games or whatever other indulgence 'floats their boat'. Sometimes I stayed awake making longer-term plans. My whole Thailand experience was formulated and booked during an evening and the whole of the next day while I was holed up in a motel in Cromwell, New Zealand, waiting for the rain to stop.

Overall, I am satisfied with the balance that emerged of different types of evening company. I was glad I had made such efforts to arrange accommodation with friends of friends or Servas hosts. My alone time was also important, presenting the opportunity to reflect, plan and write. Sometimes it was a relief to relax in my own space after a full-on time in company, and at other times (especially after ten consecutive days in hostels in New Zealand), I was glad to meet another new person and enjoy interesting conversation.

Alone and intrepid

There were times when travelling alone (especially when doing something physical) allowed me to feel intrepid. Here I was, self-motivated and miles from home, under my own steam. Cycling separately from the group along New Zealand's remote Otago Rail Trail gave a real sense of freedom. Hiring my own bike and exploring Easter Island, Aitutaki and the lake in Taupō, New Zealand, put me in complete charge of my being. Climbing the small extinct volcano on Easter Island alone (having rejected the tourist office's recommendations to employ a guide) proved to be an easy and enjoyable stroll. Even sitting on a bus and looking out on totally new places excited me. These moments made me feel alive and exhilarated, that I was experiencing the world full-on.

I spent Christmas 2019 alone in a hostel in Taupō, North Island, New Zealand. On Christmas Day I decided to be gentle with myself and try my first proper exercise after a chest infection. So in the morning I cycled a rolling three miles to Huka Falls, a local beauty spot with waterfalls and rapids – and felt good for it. It looked like rain, so I returned promptly to Taupō. But the rain held off, so I carried on around the edge of the lake along a paved walkway, enjoying the scenery. Hunger for some kind of Christmas dinner eventually kicked in. Hmm – do I go back to the hostel (alone) and virtuously eat yet more salad (alone), or do I splash out on some pork ribs at a crowded pavement café...? I didn't wonder for very long. ('No-brainer', do I hear you say?) The ribs won out, accompanied by a cocktail and then a brandy. It was a sumptuous Christmas dinner – as I felt I'd earnt it – brightened by a jovial waitress. Back at the hostel, I received some Christmas emails and WhatsApps from friends and family, and video calls with Sue, Janine, Helen (just moved to Lancaster) and Cathy. I enjoyed my very different Christmas, enhanced by unpredictable events and a fabulous, indulgent lunch.

I celebrated New Year, unaccompanied, in Wellington. It was good to spend the evening in my hotel room (so nice to have a bit of luxury after three hostels) with a huge homemade tuna and avocado salad, an equally huge G&T, and the telly. Managing to stay awake to let in 2020, I went down to the harbour to see the fireworks. It was a happy spectacle, enriched with New Year wishes from Cathy and Helen (at 11am in the UK) and from Janine in Australia, who still had two hours to wait. Though physically alone at times when I would normally have been in the thick of celebrations with friends, it was good to exchange messages with special friends and to know that people cared. This felt more caring and genuine than celebrating New Year in a bar with random strangers. And I was pleased with myself for enjoying New Year solo.

Unpredictable, casual encounters

In general, meeting people was haphazard. I left the UK hoping to form fleeting friendships with other travellers – another reason to prefer public transport to driving alone. I started my trip ready to converse with almost anyone and recognised enthusiastically any opportunities to connect. I was also ready to form deeper friendships with people I met on group adventures. In reality, the conversations I had and the friendships I made depended on sheer luck and energy levels, and few were lasting.

My memories of several random conversations stand out. Sitting on a plane to Phoenix, Arizona, the American man between me and the window showed interest in my travels and shared his political views (the opposite of mine, so I kept schtum) before helpfully pointing out details of the landscape as we came in to land. I liked him despite his politics and appreciated his kind introduction to Phoenix. It was an enjoyable conversation but could never be a friendship.

At a stop in Santa Fe, while awaiting the bus to Taos, I met a woman in her early twenties from Philadelphia. I stifled a giggle at the sight of her battling with a large rucksack and several smaller bags as well as a wide-brimmed hat under one arm and a blanket that trailed on the ground behind her – in stark contrast to my two simple bags. Our age difference was no obstacle, and she told me about her life and her journey to volunteer in a religious community beyond Taos. Towards the end of our journey we fell silent, and as we alighted, she presented me with an abstract floral design carrying the caption: *Rosie, luminous blessings on your travels*. I was touched by her kindness. Our bubbles had collided gently and bounced apart, moving on to new experiences.

Another time I was queuing to check in for my flight to Alice Springs. When I told the white Australian next to me about my interest in finding out more about Aboriginal culture, he launched into a racist tirade, so I pointedly turned my attention to my travel documents.

I had a fascinating day trip from Cairns to the mountain town of Kuranda and have vivid memories of three Texan women, one called Connie, whom I met at the end of the day in the descending cable car. We shared the usual travel histories, but I was touched by their religious zeal and the sincere warmth of their blessings as we parted.

In the Cook Islands the cultural differences sparked my curiosity, and I sensed a welcoming openness amongst the people. Out on a bike ride around the coast of Aitutaki, every local person greeted me warmly with a big smile and their customary 'Kiaorana!' A smile was usually enough to start a chat, and I met several people while eating sashimi (raw tuna) at roadside cafés. One of these chance meetings was with Liz and Brian, who made my 67th birthday so special. We had the opportunity to move beyond the 'preliminaries', and I learned from them about some underlying discrimination 'games' against whites, and how being a nurse had helped their part-Māori friend, Ciara, gain acceptance in Aitutaki. I still consider them friends and would feel welcome to look them up if I returned – but this type of lasting friendship seldom arose through chance encounters.

My main conclusion about these random encounters is that they were best appreciated in the present moment because they seldom led further. I discovered quite quickly that my capacity for initiating small talk with complete strangers was limited – 'Here we go again!' A pattern developed: we exchanged opening comments about, for example, the weather or the time we had spent queuing, soon followed by details of our respective journeys. People were often interested in the scale of my grand plan, and I would find myself describing my route for the nth time, which became tedious. Passing the time thus seldom led to friendships and in westernised countries much that was said was – dare I say? – destined to bore me, because there was no time to go deeper. Before long I ceased to initiate these conversations, but was always willing to respond politely.

Small-group travel
and unchosen company

Group travel was different again, depending on who else had booked. Apart from my three-week Peru trip, when much of my time was spent with Cathy, none of my small-group holidays lasted more than five days. For me, this was long enough to discover whose company I enjoyed and short enough to escape at the end if necessary. I always enjoyed getting to know each of my co-travellers, but it was good to know I could withdraw from the evening conversation (and even go to bed) if I felt the need. The only occasion when I had to bite my lip was on a well-organised cycling trip (by Off The Rails) along the Otago

Rail Trail, a 150-mile disused railway in New Zealand, which offered excellent opportunities to explore the history of the gold rush. Some fellow travellers displayed racist attitudes to a Japanese waitress – they doubted (wrongly) that she would understand when someone requested gluten-free. I summoned my tolerance in Peru when, travelling for long hours in the minibus, there was incessant, loud conversation between two men, and when a 14-year-old girl fed aggressive disco music through the bus's Bluetooth system. (I could say my oldfogeyness was seriously tested at these times!) But overall, I found the benefits of small-group travel outweighed the challenges. It was good to share impressions of new places, and to support each other if the terrain demanded it. Conversation was always optional.

My small-group trips to Yosemite and Tahoe, the Grand Canyon, Australia's Red Centre and the Otago Rail Trail enabled me to visit both the most celebrated tourist sights and some very remote areas without having to research and plan the detail. The longer Peru tour was superb and offered these benefits in a country where we would have had to spend hours, probably days, finding out for ourselves how to plan the same journey, and where many gems would have otherwise been beyond our reach. It also ensured that we were safe throughout; it felt good to be escorted through jungle terrain by the local police on our way to a landing stage in the Amazon basin. I would adopt the same approach to specific tourist destinations if I chose to travel again – though I have stayed in touch with not one of my fellow travellers.

For me, the balance between company and alone time was important. I appreciated the mix of situations I experienced. Despite being an only child, I found my time alone to be, in general, more challenging than my time in company, and I had to adapt to it. I think the challenge of being alone for long periods has helped me to appreciate my own space, in moderation. But I usually say 'yes' to company, and enjoy the balance with my alone time. I can still feel lonely when I'm tired and can't find the energy to occupy myself. That is the time for a good book, a good film or simply a good sleep.

GOING FOR IT AND MANAGING RISK

Mark Zuckerberg, who made his fortune by founding Facebook, said: 'The biggest risk is not taking any risk... In a world that is changing really quickly, the only strategy that is guaranteed to fail is not taking risks.'

How true! No way could I continue with the 'same old' life, so I had to accept the risks involved. What became crucial was how I would manage and calculate risk in any new circumstances. When I talk about my solo journey, people often tell me I'm brave. I think this is meant as a compliment, which I appreciate. However, I do not feel brave. The planning didn't require me to pluck up courage, and it was impossible to anticipate any difficult challenges which required bravery. If I sensed danger while travelling solo, self-preservation was needed more than bravery. I faced many risks; the important thing was to manage them.

To date – touch wood – I have been lucky with personal safety. Despite some foolish risks in my youth (including some bad decisions when hitchhiking), I now feel competent enough in calculating risk, and my antennae are sensitised to potential danger. I recognised that as a solo woman traveller I could, at times, be vulnerable and that I needed to be mindful of safety. So my plans were all within my safety 'comfort zone', and I remained ready to change the plans if necessary. The fact that Cathy would always know where I was staying also gave me security. On a trip of this scale, I didn't want unnecessary stress. Some of you readers might have taken more risks, some fewer. What mattered to me was to feel at ease with my plans. To me, it was worth the effort to clarify my ideas about how much risk I could handle without undue stress.

Alcohol

Now I am older I usually limit my alcohol intake. I still love to put my feet up with a G&T, ice and lemon, lovingly mixed by my own (fair?) hand in a very fine, large globe. I can hear the clink of ice now... Bliss! I rarely fancy wine (except bubbly) and my body usually tells me it's had enough after one pint of beer. If I drink regularly, the weight piles on. After consuming even small amounts of alcohol I malfunction the next day; it takes me longer to do a quick crossword, and my motor coordination goes to pot. I play the wrong strings out of tune on the cello, and the walls of the house visibly cringe. For the best travel experience, I wanted to maintain my fitness and hone my senses, and of course it was important to be 'on the ball' to ensure my safety. So, I decided that I would drink alcohol only in trusted company and in small quantities. As I spent a lot of time alone, this meant I drank very little. I think this was a good decision. I did, however, slip a little when I arrived at the home of one Servas host who immediately presented me with a large glass of red. We had some real belly laughs, but I paid for it with brain fog the next day out and about in the city. I got away with much greater alcohol intake with my family in Adelaide, who always drank bubbly.

Backup plans

For extra security with accommodation, I always backed up Servas arrangements with cancellable hotel bookings. Hosts, some of whom were very elderly, might need to cancel for many reasons, and I felt safe knowing I had an alternative. It was easy to check with Servas hosts a day or two beforehand whether it was still OK to visit.

Staying safe... Did I? A risk too far?

I've had some practice with staying safe (for example, using a burglar alarm when I lived in London, and travelling alone), so I used that experience while I was away. I have useful habits, such as keeping the door locked to block intruders and avoiding walking through notorious urban areas after dark.

San Francisco's shadier parts: I realised while travelling that another way to keep myself safe was to trust any sense of fear when it arose. This helped twice in San Francisco. My Servas host lived a bus ride from the city centre. One afternoon I was mentally tired from exploring but had just enough physical energy to walk all the way 'home'. En route I suddenly realised, with too little energy remaining to take a detour, that I was headed straight through the Tenderloin – a part of downtown San Francisco which I knew had poverty, drug problems and a high crime rate. Across the road I saw a person (alive or dead?) sprawled across the sidewalk; passers-by simply sidestepped. So, I made sure my valuables were zipped away safely and strode out, avoiding all eye contact until I was safely away from this downtrodden area. Another time, I was headed on foot with my luggage from a subway station towards a B&B. It was beginning to get dark. The seemingly endless wide roads were lined with identical small, grey houses, and all the cars parked unevenly on the sidewalk had seen better days. I had underestimated the distance and was beginning to lose confidence in Google Maps. I needed help but there were few people about. Intuitively trusting a passing young man, who I thought was probably a student, I asked for directions. Luckily for me, he escorted me to the B&B over the next twenty minutes while we enjoyed a pleasant chat. On reflection, I'm convinced he was looking after my safety; I might have been in more danger than I'd realised!

Lifts from strangers: In childhood I was warned never to accept lifts from strangers. Yet during my travels I sometimes found myself being driven from a station or airport in a private car. I told myself that someone meeting me with my name on a card was probably a safe bet, and chose to risk the quality of their driving. It was different one warm, sunny day in Moorea, a small island in French Polynesia. I was walking along a road in my tatty vest and shorts when a smart and prestigious, but unknown, car drew up alongside me. The well-dressed, white and apparently respectable woman driver offered me a lift, out of the blue. A kind and friendly French woman? A bored, rich widow? A madam from a brothel? Somehow, on that particular occasion, I sniffed the air, declined politely and chose not to find out. But on my 67th birthday, on Aitutaki in the Cook Islands, I disregarded all my dad's safety rules. Liz and Brian, a friendly local couple I'd met in an outdoor café, had offered to pick me up at my bungalow and take me out for a birthday meal. My opening paragraph describes what happened next. My 67th birthday was second to none. I had the most wonderfully exotic and memorable evening with a delicious meal and an island show, under the stars, of Māori music and dancing. And yes, there were grass skirts! I had met Liz and Brian previously so had already begun to trust them and their Aitutaki lifestyle. At no time did I feel endangered, and Liz's friend Ciara dropped me off safely at my bungalow. What a birthday! Sorry, Dad!

These examples show, I hope, that when travelling, decisions about personal safety are sometimes not straightforward, and calculated risks can be necessary. I have no regrets about my birthday pillion ride, and I still wonder whether refusing the lift on Moorea might have denied me an enjoyable experience.

Friends' well-meant warnings: There was one particular risk that I feel I mismanaged. Before my departure I had lunch with a well-meaning friend who is a passionate volcanologist. When I described my planned route, her comment was: 'Rosie, you aren't going to Seattle are you? I would never set foot in that area!' This was followed by a stark warning that Seattle was expected, imminently, to suffer a major earthquake and a tsunami which would submerge much of the city. After further research, I understood something of the tectonic danger to the whole western seaboard of the USA and Southwest Canada. Foolishly or wisely (I know not which), I allowed this knowledge to undermine my peace of mind while I was in that area, and my worry caused me to adjust my plans, keeping my time on the Pacific coast to a minimum. I therefore missed out on some of the more remote islands and even cancelled a Servas stay near Puget Sound, the stretch of ocean directly next to Seattle. I will leave it to you to decide how much notice I should have taken of my volcanologist friend.

Language questions: On reflection, the countries I visited made travelling relatively safe – even though these decisions were not primarily in the interests of safety. Peru, Chile (which governs Easter Island) and French Polynesia were the only countries where English was not the first language. In Peru I was on a small-group tour and with Cathy, which meant I was not alone, and my tourist Spanish was adequate. On Easter Island many people spoke English, so being alone there felt safe. I speak some French so enjoyed practising it in French Polynesia. I therefore felt that language was unlikely to present any problems – though it had to be considered. The biggest difficulty was probably learning to say 'tomaydoes' in Albuquerque.

The benefits of bus travel...?: Well, of course it's safe to travel by bus... Isn't it? Ironically my safety ploy of using buses wasn't foolproof, as I discovered on a seven-hour Greyhound bus journey from Flagstaff, Arizona, to Albuquerque in New Mexico. Getting on the bus, I noticed that the Black passengers sat towards the rear and the others towards the front. Before starting the engine the burly, unsmiling white driver made an announcement which boiled down to 'Don't mess with me!' So, I was aware of the threat of aggression. I was boarding the bus again after a toilet stop when I was pushed from behind and told menacingly by one passenger, 'You get out of my way, cos you're weak!' I think he assumed I was male because of my short hair and baseball cap, and took a dislike to me. Feeling vulnerable, rather than continue to sit alone, I moved to an empty seat beside a woman of apparently Hispanic origin. Though we spoke different languages I think she understood when I tried to explain my seat move, and I gave her some ibuprofen when she complained of a headache. We spent the rest of the journey in simple, friendly conversation and a warm silence. I got off the bus in the dark at the Albuquerque terminus, but there was no sign of Kerry, who I was expecting to pick me up. Soon very few strangers from the bus remained and all was quiet. I felt alone and vulnerable. Just as I was beginning to concoct a plan B, headlights finally appeared and Kerry arrived. You could say I was relieved!

My faith in buses was challenged again in New Mexico, on the road from Santa Fe to Taos. The (free) bus was extremely old and almost empty, and I sat at the back with my fellow traveller and her chaotic luggage so we had a view out both left and right. A lap belt prevented my head from hitting the roof over bumps, making it a luxurious journey (not!). About twenty miles from Taos, the bus was diverted – something about a fire. The diversion took us along the 'old' road – fine for a while if tortuous and hilly – until I saw a precarious-looking bridge ahead and a chatty passenger held up his hand with fingers crossed. Still in one piece after rattling across the bridge, I saw the road degenerate into a rutted gravel track, steeper and more winding, along the precipitous side of a mountain – and this old bus was designed for urban roads! So I clung fearfully to the seat in front, to give the safety belt some moral support and waited for the rear axle to break. Luckily it held and we bounced and swerved for about two miles before the tarmac resumed. The bonus from this unnerving episode was that we had fabulous views of the Rio Grande in its gorge (still very full-flowing) and crossed the gorge again (by a decent bridge) at a scenic point where the river was starkly and deeply incised. We arrived in Taos only twenty minutes late.

These were not the only times when, having believed my plan was foolproof, I experienced risks I hadn't anticipated. My experience in Moorea, which I describe later as a low point of my travels, illustrates this.

Regrets?: Safety considerations did, however, limit how I travelled and the more detailed decisions about where I went. I was aware of the remoteness of the Pacific Islands and didn't want to be stranded there or be too distant from medical services. The airports are located on the busiest islands, so for a more authentic and rural experience in both French Polynesia and the

Cook Islands, I planned time on smaller islands which still had good connections with the main airport. Feeling brave, I took a boat to Moorea in French Polynesia, and in the Cook Islands a plane to Aitutaki, 124 miles from the capital. What I hadn't realised (owing to inadequate research) was that to find more traditional communities I would have needed the time and flexibility to travel even further, and more slowly, to more isolated places. Though my trip to Aitutaki was wonderful in other ways, I never experienced truly traditional communities in the Pacific (if indeed they still exist). Throughout my travels on land, unless I was on an organised tour, I usually used public transport, especially buses, in the belief that this would be safe. So I rarely found myself in remote places or far away from major roads. These self-imposed safety restrictions brought me the closest I have been to regret. I compromised my journey for the sake of safety and a full itinerary. I still wonder how it would have been for me, to risk spending more time amongst the most isolated Cook Islands people. Perhaps I'll go back...?

As a solo woman in her late 60s, my safety as a long-distance traveller had to be a consideration – but that is true for anyone of any age. I realised that stepping out of the ordinary would inevitably carry an element of risk, which I did my best to calculate. Usually it felt right; occasionally I veered towards overcautious; occasionally I slipped or didn't predict all eventualities. Doing something new always involves risk, and I don't believe it's possible to get it right all the time. The only way of avoiding risk was to do nothing, which wasn't an option for me. In fact, I believe that not travelling would have carried equal or greater risk. Accepting more of that same old life, and therefore missing opportunities to tick off some items on the bucket list, would have been stultifying. This is not good for mental health. Nor is harbouring regrets – which would have been huge if I had rejected the challenge to travel. Domestic accidents, such as falls, increase with age, so it could not be assumed that travel was more risky than staying at home. And staying at home with the same old habits would almost certainly have made me 'old before my time'.

What is in no doubt is that I am continually glad I found the confidence and determination to carry out my plan, risks included. Every day, in some small way, I celebrate the journey I made to be where I am now.

STUFF MATTERS!

No one wants their belongings damaged or stolen, but as a traveller this became even more important to me. My holdall and daysack were the only tangible source of permanence in my ever-changing world. I thought it would help me to keep track of things if I carried the minimum number of bags.

Possessions

Yes, I'd come away ready for change and excited by the idea that 'anything could happen', but I was surprised at myself when I realised how much my stuff began to matter. It was always a huge relief when it surfaced in baggage reclaim. After disembarking from the seaplane on Vancouver Island, I took a photo of my holdall, with its distinctive red strap, being unloaded from the tiny hold. Seeing this in my blog, Cathy remarked (semi-humorously) that I was becoming overly attached to my luggage. She was spot on! Fortunately luck was with me: my bag always found its way from check-in to the same flight as me, and I rejoiced when it miraculously appeared on the reclaim conveyor afterwards.

Unexpectedly, bus travel put my bag at greater risk. A bag the size of mine always had to go in the luggage hold. Somewhere in New Zealand most people were getting off at a larger town and only a few of us were travelling onward. The driver had parked the bus, so everyone alighted for refreshments. While returning to the bus, I decided to check that my bag was still on board. Surprise, surprise: it was looking forlorn, abandoned and neglected on the tarmac after everyone else had reclaimed theirs. Good job I checked!

Money

I tried not to carry large amounts of cash. Plastic was accepted widely, and I had a card which allowed me to withdraw from ATMs free of charge. I took as much care of my valuables as I would anywhere in the UK. As well as wearing clothes with large, zipped pockets, I carried a money belt which stayed next to my skin during major journeys. I am by nature quite careful and vigilant, so this worked well most of the time, but I had a mishap one day when I was tired.

In my money belt I carried US$400 in cash for emergencies, planning to spend whatever was left in Thailand, my final destination. At the end of any journey, I transferred my money belt to my daysack and kept it with me permanently. Or so I thought. One day I decided to check on my cash for Thailand – and it wasn't there! Or anywhere! With untold angst I racked my brain for any memories of having exchanged it, and mentally retraced my steps to find any explanation of how it had gone missing.

The only answer I could think of took me back to my single room in a hostel in New Zealand. By mistake I had left my money belt in my daysack in my locked room in a hostel and gone out without it for the evening. On my return I checked that the belt was still there, but I didn't check the contents. The rather creepy warden would have had a key to my room, and coincidentally during the evening, I had bumped into him in a bar where he had obviously had a few too many. With hindsight I believe he had searched my bag and helped himself. This theft remained undiscovered for weeks. The loss of the money was annoying and inconvenient, but far worse was the stress I gave myself trying to find an explanation, and the mental bruises I gave myself after beating myself up for being careless. It was a hard lesson in staying alert, however tired I might be.

SECTION 4:
TRAVELLING – SOME MAGICAL
(AND NOT-SO-MAGICAL) MOMENTS

Throughout my travels, I sought to tune in to all of the sights, sounds and smells I encountered, and to be open to whatever emotions arose in response. What struck me was the diversity of our world and how precarious it is. There were times when I was utterly blown away – ample reward for travelling those long distances. Some experiences took my mind out of focus so that all I could say was 'Wow!' Words are still inadequate to convey my feelings at those times. Bad times were few – but also noteworthy. Here are just a few of my most memorable experiences of the places I visited. Many of the memories now feel surreal, though the moments as I lived them were vivid and very real. All of them had an impact on my awareness and, indirectly, on my way forward. To bring these moments back to life, I describe them using the present tense.

BRITISH COLUMBIA, CANADA: A WELCOMING FIRST STOP

Vancouver

I have come to meet Samuel, a First Nation citizen introduced to me by my friend Rose. He has invited me to a fast-food café in a shabby part of Vancouver, where roads seem to matter more than people. Using Google Maps to find it takes me through an unmanicured, semi-residential area where tourists seldom tread. It's a familiar feeling, like searching for an obscure shop in a rundown part of London. The first thing he says is, 'Hey, I'm sorry we're meeting here, but at least I know they will serve me.' He explains about the racism he often encounters, and that challenging it is futile. Samuel is a quiet, mild-mannered, peace-loving, native Cree speaker dressed in a padded check shirt and jeans. He gives me a copy of *Megaphone* magazine, similar to the British *Big Issue*, which he sometimes sells. It contains a poem which he has written about homelessness in Vancouver.

We take a walk through the economically deprived Hastings area of downtown Vancouver, where he rents a small apartment that he is proud to show me. It's a converted tenement block where he has a bedsit with basic comforts, plus a door that locks securely – worth celebrating for someone who has had to sleep rough. We take a short boat trip to a specialist mineral and rock shop where he buys materials to make a dream catcher, which he will sell to contribute to his income. As we get to know each other he generously tells me about some of his struggles, amongst them homelessness. He now has a varied life which, as well as selling *Megaphone*, includes teaching the Cree language, assisting with home removals and mentoring ex-convicts. We enjoy each other's company, and I feel honoured to spend a pleasant and fascinating day with him. I am touched when, as a parting gift, he gives me a tiny red package like the salt that used to come in a packet of crisps. This talisman is designed to protect me on my journey.

In a café in central Vancouver I meet Henry, also a First Nation citizen. With his long black hair in a plait, he is conspicuous. Worried about racism, he is almost hidden behind the screen of his laptop in a corner of the café. 'Oh, hi. You must be Rosie. I'm glad you made it cos I won't be thrown out if I'm with a white woman.' This is another saddening lesson for me. We spend a very enjoyable two hours finding we share many values, and I hear, again, about the challenges of being a First Nation Vancouverite, and the prejudice he suffers.

Both of these men, through their own determination and fortitude, have made huge improvements in their lifestyles – and I admire them for the work they now do to support others less fortunate. But many First Nation people still live in poverty, and racism is rife. Canada celebrates and proudly exhibits artefacts created by people of the First Nations, and in particular totem poles. Huge ones are displayed in Vancouver's Museum of Anthropology, and there are some in Stanley Park. They are also prominent features on Newcastle Island near Nanaimo and on Hornby Island. Colourful. Striking. Artistic. But they do not, in themselves, tell the full story.

All of the above is a stark backdrop to my time in a very wealthy part of Canada. Vancouver is a city of luxury and great beauty, where property prices are exorbitant. The natural world is always in evidence, even in the city. Some cute, small turtles live in Vancouver's Stanley Park Lake (with Canada geese also in profusion). I enjoy a rare sighting of a pod of orcas in the Strait of Georgia and suddenly find myself six feet away from a large owl in wooded parkland. Dinah and I climb the Grouse Grind, a forested and relentless steep climb of 2,624 feet. A *grind* it is, and very humbling – Wansfell, near Ambleside, a mere pimple by comparison. Dinah (fit as a flea) has gone on ahead, and I feel daunted as I rest and sip coconut water. Yes, Rosie, you're going to finish this and not give up! So I tackle the next stage of this forbidding, upward slog. I finally reach the top, exhausted, sweating cobs and gasping for breath, and find Dinah cool and serene after her half-hour wait. She's a tough cookie! Once I recover, I am rewarded and awed by a stunning southward view across the whole of Vancouver, which is followed by a perfect ice cream and an expertly served beer.

Visiting Vancouver Island gives me my first ever chance to take a seaplane – an expense I haven't anticipated, but when else will I have a similar opportunity? I stand on the quay and watch, fascinated, while my luggage is stowed in the minute hold before departure. I feel apprehensive as I embark – will this thing actually *fly*? – but I tell myself this is a routine service and utterly normal for many commuters. The tiny plane is noisy and cramped with about fourteen passengers, without even the headspace to stand erect. As we take off from the water's surface, the windows are drenched with spray, which obliterates any view, and we seem to bob up and down, buffeted mercilessly by air currents. Once aloft, the journey becomes smooth and I have rewarding views of a silvery Strait of Georgia, with its visibly intermingling currents, and the complicated coastlines of several islands, through a hazy sun. Along comes one of those 'I'm intrepid' feelings and I grin to myself. We land in the water (is that possible?) and dock safely in Victoria, and I watch again happily while my bag is unloaded by hand and given directly to me – no luggage trailers or conveyors here! A joyful reunion.

Denman Island

Denman Island, in the Strait of Georgia, is my ultimate Canadian destination. I travel north by bus from Victoria, alight with curiosity in what seems an unlikely and nondescript spot with a café, and find a chain ferry which takes me to the island. It is hard to believe, as I near my destination, that this remote island can host an esoteric, classical musical event with world-class tutors flown in from Italy. Andrew, one of the organisers, greets me with a bear hug, announcing, 'We hug here on Denman.' So much for formality! We walk in the sun to the local café. I am undecided whether he or his partner, Robert, looks more like Gandalf. Musicians and producers from Canada and the US, along with several Europeans, are meeting for a week to rehearse from scratch and perform Henry Purcell's opera *The Fairy-Queen*. Andrew even, very generously, lends me his cello! The rehearsals are fun but disciplined, and it is a joy to play cello again with other musicians. For the first time, I also get my hands on a lirone and a rebek – rare period instruments which others have brought.

Coming together with musicians from Europe and North America shows me the power of the international language of music and the common culture shared by Western classical musicians regardless of nationality. Socially, Denman Baroque feels identical to musical events in England – a 'home from home' experience – and I receive several invitations to visit people in the northern US. The final performance in the village hall, held in the afternoon to allow people to make the return journey in one day, draws an audience of over a hundred and is a great success. There is a party on the final evening, and I feel totally at ease.

When not ensconced in the music I have time to experience Denman – where friendliness and hospitality are second to none. Denman is known as the Canadian

Riviera, with its mild climate and gentle environment. The atmosphere is utterly laid back. Local people show concern for the environment and many grow their own produce. A cinnamon-like aroma perfuses the evening air. My kind and generous hosts, Anne and Rick, show me round, introduce me to friends and organise the loan of a bike. Through them I meet many local people and begin to understand life in this remote community. During my explorations I am reminded of the hippy past of the island. The local estate agency is housed in a 'gypsy' caravan, and a local dignitary nurses on her lap a healthy cannabis plant (legal in Canada). Another first for me on Denman is the gloopy fun of trying a potter's wheel, thanks to Jeanie, who makes soulful and elegant creations.

Hornby Island

Hornby Island is even more remote, reached only by ferry from Denman. I have heard about The Fabricators, a group of women who meet regularly to spin and weave, so one rainy morning I go to investigate. I find them in their own workshop premises, a small, wooden hall filled with hand looms and spinning wheels, with wool and yarn at various stages of processing. The natural colours and vividly dyed skeins are an uplifting sight during the wet, grey weather. The women's welcome is warm, and while they card, spin and weave, they seem to enjoy telling me about what they are doing – while also wanting to hear my story. After this heartwarming two hours, I buy a vegan meal from a catering caravan (the only eatery which is open) and devour it at a trestle table. I have already been struck by Hornby Island's raw and wild coastal beauty, with the aroma of pine needles, the omnipresent driftwood logs and sky-scraping trees. The rain stops, so I take a walk along a coastal trail which is fresh and vibrant from the morning's downpour. I find myself standing still to open my senses; to capture the experience I take photos and make a few notes. Later, alone in my B&B, I am pleasantly surprised when this poem comes together:

FOREST

Moist, alive, resuscitated by the gift of rain,
Fresh foliage vibrant, moss and leaf-mould dripping joy.
Small creatures, emerging from their homes in bark, celebrate refreshment.
Footfall soft on pine- and fir-clad, perfumed earth,

The crunch of twigs, the creak of tall, tall fir and
cedar.

Pat PAT! as drops, from highest treetops
blown,

Drum greetings lower, on maple leaves and
fern.

And shy, brown birds find refuge in the lower
leaves –

Not for them the canopy, where ravens dip and
dodge

Teased truculently by crows.

Shoreline forest breathing hiss of shingle,

Ocean tugging back with breaking wave –

Softly recalling previous powerful storms

Which heaved their drifted trunks,

To drop them, in the aftermath, along the shore.

Conglomerate boulders, black-green from
ancient times

Poised to tumble yet again when gravity
dictates,

And the free, unruly geometry of fallen trees

Resting now, with love and purpose new.

And here, my friend, you might choose to build
your cabin.

After leaving Hornby, I have another gratifying experience. Back on Denman I realise I've left my travel adaptor at the B&B on Hornby. I ring the B&B and yes, they have found it and will arrange for it to be returned to me. In the event, my B&B host meets the ferry the next time it docks and hands the adaptor to the ferry operator. I cycle to meet the ferry when it arrives at Denman and receive my adaptor along with a big smile. The joys of island life!

The kindness and generosity I receive in British Columbia at the start of my travels affect me deeply. I feel enriched and awed by the goodwill I have experienced everywhere as a total stranger, and this fuels my reflection, in more general terms, on human beings' capacity for loving kindness. Canada also presents me with contradictions which I struggle to reconcile: kind and generous people living alongside huge inequalities of wealth, and passive acceptance of the endemic racism towards First Nation people.

THE AMERICAN SOUTHWEST: LAND OF ENCHANTMENT AND KINDNESS

San Francisco

The song 'San Francisco' by Scott McKenzie reached UK number one in 1967. Despite my traditional upbringing, the song's instructions about wearing some flowers in your hair appealed to my free-spirited alter ego. Now, sitting in a street-corner coffee bar in Haight-Ashbury, San Francisco, I wallow in discovering a key venue from the origins of hippiedom, and a café which Ernest Hemingway had frequented. Since my teens, I have been attracted to the West Coast of the US – thanks to the era of the Beach Boys and Joni Mitchell, which gave me a sense of rebellion, fun and flower power. In 1967 I tried to be a part-time hippy with white loon pants, bare feet, flowers and a bell hanging round my neck, but I also had to stay in and do my homework – so the fantasy had to suffice.

More recently I have become aware of some differences in outlook between inhabitants of the US

East Coast and the West. Pioneering women travelled west in the early 1900s with independence, resilience and determination to shake off what they saw as the dominant and repressive 'respectability' culture of the East Coast. For more on this, you might like to read *Ladies of the Canyons* by Lesley Poling-Kempes. And, of course, there was Georgia O'Keeffe, the free-spirited and inspiring artist from the early twentieth century, whose art captivates me. So I am very excited by my plans to visit California, Arizona and New Mexico. My visit is long overdue, and sipping an Americano in Haight-Ashbury proves I have really arrived.

For a full day, I follow the San Francisco tourist trail and appreciate its quirkiness – its hilly streets make it different from any city I have visited. It is worth queuing for ninety minutes to take the famous, crowded Hyde Street cable car up the steep hill from Fisherman's Wharf. This ancient tram slowly creaks and toils to the top, and I seriously wonder whether it will make it with its load of tourists. But it does. Then I wander along the water's edge lined with shops and food outlets, absorbing the multicultural atmosphere. I take a bus across the iconic Golden Gate Bridge and see the San Francisco skyline from across the Bay, watching the famous fog rolling in as the afternoon progresses. Just drinking in the atmosphere in Frisco puts a massive tick on the bucket list, and I am proud to be here.

El Capitan

Occasionally something on TV etches an indelible impression. I first saw a broadcast about a 3,600-foot ascent of El Capitan in Yosemite in the late 1980s. The Nose of El Capitan is a huge, solid mass of granite which challenges even the most experienced climbers. In the documentary, the climbers sleep on a ledge only two feet wide and run to and fro across the vertical rock face, swinging pendulum-like to leap to a secure base for the next stage of their climb. The documentary is exhilarating and impressive, and I marvel at the climbers' fearlessness and determination – all the more because I once tried two (but succeeded with only one) very easy rock climbs myself at Bull's Hollow near Tunbridge Wells (thanks, Mick!). Later I enjoyed *Free Solo*, about the intrepid Alex Honnold, who successfully conquered the Nose alone and unroped.

Fascinated by El Capitan, I need to see it for myself, and I am now enjoying a minibus trip to Yosemite. I stand at the bottom of the Nose, craning my neck to look up...

up... up, and I feel utterly intimidated. I am stunned by its huge size and by the geological power which must have created it. It is an unimaginably large, grey rock face which towers over the valley, majestic, ominous and forbidding even to expert climbers. One co-traveller who has a telephoto lens picks out a climber high on the rock face – hardly visible as a tiny dot on the photo I take using my mobile. One tiny climber – and all that rock! How insignificant we humans are when the world is viewed on such a grand scale! Witnessing this courageous feat firsthand in such a stunning environment has been one of the most awe-inspiring experiences of my life.

The Grand Canyon

My impressions of the Grand Canyon, also drawn mostly from TV, led me to include it in my bucket list. Something about the relentless, rocky landscape inspired me, along with dramatic Western movies set in that or similar terrain. I associate the Grand Canyon with the Wild West and a sense of unfettered freedom.

My excellent Wildland Trekking trip starts in Flagstaff, Arizona, from where the group has an eighty-mile minibus drive to the Grand Canyon's South Rim. As we rumble along I delight in seeing, for real, Arizona's huge saguaro cacti standing proud against the barren earth and blue sky. My excitement mounts as our driver takes us past some imposing mesas – those large, flat, rocky outcrops (cap rocks) with clearly defined rock strata and gentler slopes at the bottom formed by eroded, smaller stones. As the minibus approaches our first scheduled stop for a panorama of the Grand Canyon, we emerge from passive window-gazing into a highly alert state of readiness. The bushes lining the road obscure our view, until our driver slows down and tells us to prepare for a first sighting... It is a fleeting moment but so powerful! Through a gap in the bushes, I glimpse a huge expanse of rock and valley in pastel shades which are deepening in the now late afternoon. All the emotions I have unwittingly stored away from movies and TV well up, and I find my cheeks moist. Surprising myself, I have shed tears at this overwhelming, though brief, exposure. I am amazed throughout three more glorious days of walking, surrounded by that astonishing scenery, but never as much as when I caught that first glimpse. How unpredictable our emotions can be!

New Mexico

Bright yellow T-shirts from New Mexico carry the bright red slogan *Land of Enchantment*, and I am compelled to buy one. Mine is one of my most cherished souvenirs and reminds me of the state's sandy, desert terrain and the hot, raw environment. Kerry, my welcoming friend in Albuquerque, is an outdoor enthusiast. When I accept her offer to take me camping at Chaco Canyon over the summer solstice, I have no idea what to expect. But I am intrigued by the name, which suggests more experience of the Wild West, so I prepare for a magical mystery tour.

She drives for over three hours, out into desert terrain and along empty, unmetalled roads. I am surprised to experience, in this wealthy country where car-driving is taken for granted, this long, bumpy journey through an economically disadvantaged, rural area. We rumble and vibrate noisily through a desolate landscape of mesa where the rocks range in colour from pastel to deep red. Chaco Canyon is a remote area with the remains of a Native American village and a rudimentary campsite. We pitch our tents with difficulty, fighting to control the canvas as it flaps and billows in a strong, warm wind. The very dry afternoon is hot! Nearby, across the desert scrub, towering sandstone cliffs reach vertically into a cloudless, deep blue sky. The only sign of life is a majestic, lone eagle soaring overhead. Surreal! Again, I am knocked out by a sense of freedom and the once-unexplored West of the US. In my mind's eye there is a lonesome cowboy on his horse, ambling along the trail at the base of the cliff. This is one of the most enduring sensations of my whole trip.

My interest in Native American people takes me to the Taos Pueblo, a UNESCO World Heritage Site and one of the oldest existing Native American villages. It belonged originally to the Red Willow people. The Pueblo is preserved in the old tradition; its only water source is the Willow River, and there is no electricity. The buildings are adobe, a mud brick material bound by straw or grass. Any upper-storey dwellings are reached by an exterior wooden ladder. It is a starkly technologically simple village. Exploring this quiet place demands respect, and I experience a strong sense of mystery and otherworldly wisdom, wondering at the simple lifestyle which still prevails there. Today the Taos Pueblo has about seven permanently resident families. Others come seasonally or visit, and craftspeople who prefer to live outside the Pueblo arrive to sell their wares. The Pueblo is a reminder of the poverty of the Native Americans, and I get a feeling that we tourists are tolerated because the Pueblo needs income. The old, ruined San Geronimo church is surrounded by a dilapidated cemetery. I am shocked to learn that, in 1847, 150 Pueblo-dwellers were burned alive in that building by members of the US army, in retaliation for the murder of one soldier. Lest we forget!

The nearby town of Taos is struggling economically. In the early 1900s, it was an artistic centre, attracting women pioneers and visited by D.H. Lawrence and Georgia O'Keeffe. The few remaining galleries and art shops attest to its history. To me, it feels like a neglected outpost of Santa Fe. It seems that Taos is more typical of ordinary life in New Mexico, with considerable poverty in contrast with prestigious Santa Fe and commercial Albuquerque. I notice some poorly maintained public spaces, old cars and many apparently unemployed folk. Chatting to a man I meet sitting on a bench, I learn that the town is effectively bankrupt. At this time, in 2019, I have never heard that said about any towns in the UK, and I wonder, sadly, how it could have come about.

Georgia O'Keeffe expertly captured New Mexico on canvas. I was amazed by an exhibition of her work in London, so I visit Ghost Ranch, where she lived, about sixty miles north of Santa Fe, and see for real some of the vistas she painted. I am shown a copy of one of her famous landscape paintings and taken to stand in the exact spot where she must have placed her easel to reproduce what I now see before me. She had a remarkable eye for detail and made stunning use of colour. I marvel at how she captured not only the landscape but also an atmosphere. I see the house where she lived and threw parties on the roof. A strong and taciturn woman, she rejected her formal art teaching in favour of individuality of expression – a heroine to the rebellious side of my nature. A gallery dedicated to her work, in Santa Fe, aptly celebrates her unique talent.

New Mexico, and in particular my experiences of Chaco Canyon, the Taos Pueblo and Georgia O'Keeffe's Ghost Ranch, awaken again my romantic attachment to the freedom of the Wild West while also bringing me close to the earth – an unlikely but intoxicating mix of Bohemian emotions?

I came to the US full of impressions conveyed through the media, especially TV. Westerns cultivated in me a romantic sense of freedom and adventure and undoubtedly led me to the Southwest – and I am glad they did. I have been to beautiful and stunning places which demonstrate the power of nature. Another (perhaps judgemental) impression I brought with me is 'Americans are in love with their cars'. Well, yes – and with good reason. Where distances are great, populations widespread and public transport limited, the car is a practical solution. And because many of the roads are uncongested, driving is more relaxed than in the UK. There's no hurry – you can tootle along at your own pace, so a 200-mile journey is much easier to contemplate. So I can now see why, in the US, cars are so important. (I am interested to discover, later, that the same is true of Australia, though I have not picked up this impression from the media.) Through the media I have also formed some negative expectations of the US: gangsters, gun violence and frightening political views. Though I felt more exposed to this side of life in the streets of San Francisco and on my Greyhound bus, my lasting impression is of an orderly society with kind, friendly people and a seemingly genuine care for others. I am now careful not to generalise too much after being bombarded with media sensationalism.

PERU: THE EXPERIENCE!

A shaky start

Around 6 am, my flight from Santa Fe lands in grey-skied Lima. Cathy should have flown in from the UK last night, and we have arranged that she will return to the airport from her B&B and meet me at Starbucks. We haven't yet been able to organise Peruvian phone or email contact, and I have discovered that, contrary to internet information, the Lima airport's Starbucks has no public Wi-Fi. So we can't alert each other to any delays or complications, and I just have to hope the plan works out. I buy a coffee, occupy the one remaining table and sit down to wait in hope – for the whole day if necessary, though she is due to arrive by 9 am. I glance around me frequently, in case we have missed each other, and find it hard to concentrate on reading. When I am eventually engrossed in my book, a shadow falls across the table and there, unbelievably, is Cathy with her large holdall in tow – another surreal moment! I am overjoyed to greet her and enormously relieved that, after each of us has travelled from different parts of the globe to this unfamiliar Latin American airport, our rendezvous has been successful. After making sure we're not dreaming, we begin our mind-expanding adventure into the real Peru, during which every day brings new sights, sounds and smells.

Grey Lima, so-called because it lacks sunshine, must be the most soul-destroying capital city I have ever visited. In July it is heavy with cloud and traffic fumes. Brown cliffs line the promenade. I unwisely take an express bus during the rush hour – not only canned like a sardine but deafened by traffic noise and whistles and almost overcome by poor ventilation. Sorry, Peru – I know Lima is an interesting city but I will be glad to leave. After a depressing journey south through the drab, brown Lima desert, I seriously wonder why I am here!

A tiny plane over the Nazca Lines

Finally we have some respite (and a sunset!) at the resort of Paracas and thankfully knock back one or two Pisco Sours. Next day we have the opportunity to see the Nazca Lines. Nazca is a small, busy mining town with hustle and bustle, fumes and desert dust. The Nazca Lines are geoglyphs, etched into the landscape between 500 BC and 500 AD, and can only be seen properly from the air. The plane is minute, seating only six including the pilot and the (female) copilot. Taking off is scary – I have no knowledge of the safety record of these tiny planes. I am uncomfortably aware of the engine noise (despite protective earmuffs) and the buffeting of the air currents carrying us upward. But as I eventually relax into the flight, my fear turns to wonder. We see below us, permanently cut into the rock surfaces below, many straight lines as well as recognisable, ancient images of animals, including a spider and a condor. I am struck by the number and complexity of the images, and by the fact that they have survived for about 2,000 years. It is thought they were a ritual to the gods, in an effort to bring rain – such extensive and enduring evidence of human perseverance. The fear returns as the pilot brings the plane down to a bumpy landing, but I survive and queue for my souvenir passport stamp.

The wonders of Lake Titicaca

Lake Titicaca is one of the world's highest navigable lakes and forms part of the boundary between Peru and Bolivia. The high-altitude air is cold and clear, but the sun is fierce. We take a boat trip to the colourful, legendary floating island of Suma Tortora. Huge bales of golden straw are bound together to provide a large, habitable platform big enough to support a whole village and small landing stage. As the submerged straw decomposes it is replaced on the surface, forming a semi-permanent construction. The lake-dwellers live from fishing and tourism, and during our visit the women and children wear brightly coloured local costume. They take us out to other islands in a bright yellow ornamental boat with sides curved upwards fore and aft. The heat of the sun intensifies while the women row and the children entertain us with loud, rough versions of 'Alouette' and 'Row, Row, Row Your Boat' – a strangely cute and enjoyable treat in such an exotic setting. Our accommodation is at Luquina Chico on the shores of the lake. The villagers serenade us in a ceremonious welcome and take us to a playing field where we are challenged to a footie match; even I join in briefly despite a very long day! As darkness descends, they dress us, over our existing garb, in national costume (Cathy looks the part), put on some Peruvian music and teach us a folk dance. The cold of the night keeps us nimble on our feet, but I want my bed!

Only after we are completely exhausted are we taken to meet our homestay hosts Manuel, his wife Separina and his son Roger – one of the wealthier families with a good-sized farm and a flushing toilet. In bed I am weighed down by the heaviest blankets I have ever experienced – but both Cathy and I sleep well.

Over breakfast we begin to get to know the family. Their native language is Quechua, but they speak Spanish, so Cathy engages with them in detail. Listening, fascinated, I piece together an understanding of their lives and our many shared values. I mention my bucket-list ambition to milk a cow, so Manuel takes us out onto the farm. We have to bring the cow from a distant pasture. However hard I tug on its rope (with Cathy collapsing in giggles) I can't get the blessed animal to move, but with Manuel's help we manage to shift it, and he hobbles it for my safety. Then, hallelujah! I manage to produce a few squirts! (Which is enough; it is very hard on the hands.) But another tick on the bucket list – and I have come all the way to Lake Titicaca to achieve it. This does not come free of charge. Manuel then takes us to a pile of wheat stalks drying on a tarpaulin in the sun. I look around, trying to locate the combine harvester, then we realise our task is to thresh the grains by hand. Manuel equips us with stout sticks and suggests we might find a rhythm if we sing. So at 12,500 feet in the scorching Peruvian midday sun, we beat the hell out of this pile of stalks to a slow rendition of 'Yellow Submarine'. OMG, really?! But both Cathy and I feel great warmth for our Lake Titicaca homestay hosts, and we appreciate this rare opportunity to spend some 'quality time' with local people.

Rainbow Mountain

We get up at 4 am for a day trip to Rainbow Mountain, having been told it is worth the effort. The precarious three-hour drive swings us about in our seats, round the contours of several precipitous valleys. At length we arrive at a car park overrun with tourists and coaches. A few men in red attire are selling donkey rides to the top, and there are women in colourful weaves selling garments and tickets to the only loos (which, we overhear, are best avoided). The long, well-worn trail, upwards to 19,000 feet, takes us past the imposing Ausangate Glacier, but before sunup it is too cold to stop for a photo. As we near the summit, we notice the beginnings of streaks of colour in the valley sides, and the sun begins to peep over the horizon. The final ascent is unbelievable! We are surrounded, in blazing sunshine, by mountain strata striped with truly amazing and unexpected pastel shades. A worthwhile trip? In spades!

The Lares Trek – a good decision?

Rather than hike the archaeological Inca Trail to Machu Picchu we choose the Lares Trek, which, we have been told, offers more human interest. At the briefing we learn we will cross a mountain pass at 15,000 feet and spend two nights camping at 11,800 feet. It sounds challenging, but we feel intrepid so cast aside our nervousness. The High Andes are snow-capped and magnificent at the start of the trek, and the trail is similar to some of the highest on a good day in the Lake District winter. But the weather deteriorates. On the second and most challenging day of the trek there is icy-cold rain and a chilly wind, so it is impossible to stop and admire any views – not that we get many. The cooks who accompany us do their best to prepare palatable, hot food at altitude, but despite our hunger, it is difficult to stomach the hard, unsalted potatoes and heavy carbohydrates. Cathy is just recovering from diarrhoea and I have just begun with a mild dose, so we both lack energy. Our ascent is arduous and we toil at the back of the group, slowly and stolidly lifting each foot in front of the other. Several miles below the summit, a boy and mule appear, apparently from nowhere, and we are told this is the 'ambulance'. Determined to complete the climb, Cathy lightens her load by putting her rucksack on the mule's back – a timely solution! We finally reach the top of the pass in wind-driven sleet, so we hurriedly take a photo, then immediately begin our descent. The only word we can find to describe that ascent is 'gruelling'. Frankly, owing to the weather, the Lares Trek has been a hard slog rather than a wonderful scenic experience – though we do have a sense of achievement.

The camping is easier than anticipated. Our tents are already erected when we arrive, and as long as we wear everything we have with us and stay zipped cosily into our four-season sleeping bags, we are warm enough and very soon comatose. I later awake struggling with the need to wee and the attempt to hold on until morning, and I finally admit defeat. But I have a problem: no way am I going out into that mind-numbingly cold mountain night, so I have to find another solution while Cathy sleeps on. Fond of alternative technology, I have a brainwave! I remember saving a large, empty crisp packet and discover that, if positioned carefully and held tightly in place, it can be filled from a kneeling position. Oh, the relief! It goes on for ages, but the trusty bag contains all of it, and I lodge it under the flysheet until morning. My rummaging, of course, wakes Cathy (it is a very small tent). Hearing the sound of running water she can hardly believe what I am up to. I am wickedly proud of my discovery, though it leaves Cathy wondering what I might do next. Needing a wee herself (and lacking a crisp packet) she chooses to brave the night air and returns enthralled after seeing a crystal-clear, starlit sky. Happy campers both, we manage a few more hours' sleep, and the next morning the flysheet (and the crisp bag) are frozen solid.

On our descent from the pass, we visit a small homestead in a valley – a single storey built of stone to withstand the weather. As it's Saturday, two young girls are at home. Their weekday walk to school in the nearest town normally takes ninety minutes each way. They sit next to cooking pots by an open hearth. Guinea pigs, soon to be cooked and eaten, run around the floor and live under the bed. The girls seem content, and our guide tells us they are materially poor but spiritually rich. I don't know whether to feel embarrassed; here are we, a bunch of relatively wealthy outsiders, descending on local people whose lives cannot be easy – but they are welcoming.

The Lares Trek has been varied and challenging but my mixed feelings remain. I cannot pretend I enjoy outdoor life in all weathers. With the unpalatable food

I have found most of the trek a physical struggle – and I am not a natural camper. It has been a memorable, if testing, experience of the Andes.

Machu Picchu

We take a bus to Machu Picchu. Despite having seen many famous media images, I am astonished when I reach the Sun Gate and take in the stunning view: perfectly engineered stone buildings positioned meticulously over a vast expanse of steep and inhospitable terrain and set against imposing mountains. Built by the Incas around 1450 AD, Machu Picchu still survives almost intact. It is awe-inspiring to see this place for real, to learn about the powerful Inca Empire and society, and to have the freedom to wander at will.

The Amazon jungle

Towards the end of our tour, we are taken to the Amazon basin and the mighty Tambopata River. The drive through banana plantations to the embarcadero, or landing stage, is in itself an experience: we travel in convoy with police escorts, presumably for our protection, from whom or what I know not. On board, we chug noisily and powerfully along the centre of the huge, jungle-lined river for two hours as darkness falls. In the first twenty minutes, we see red and green macaws, a juvenile caiman on the riverbank and a family of capybaras, rodents like three-feet-long guinea pigs. Then along comes rain, accompanied by distant thunder. I feel I am in an alien and inhospitable world, and it is a relief when the translucent plastic sheets at the sides of the boat are lowered to keep us dry, though they limit visibility. This is another surreal experience – to be on a tributary to the Amazon, approaching our riverside accommodation by boat in heavy rain and with darkness approaching. The next day our opportunities to see wildlife are hampered by the persistent rain, but we feed crackers to some piranhas and have good views of howler monkeys swinging through trees. Scavenging around the dining room at the lodge are agoutis – spaniel-sized rodents with small heads, large bellies and cheeky personalities. Filling my senses here are the constant noises from a variety of animals, the humidity and the rich gentleness of the environment. Though the forest is not being denuded in these parts, national park wardens still work with environmentalists to prevent illegal gold mining and logging, and to maintain the fragile ecological balance.

Alone again, with time to reflect

Cathy and I spend some extra days in Cusco at the end of our tour – preferable, by far, to Lima. Cusco was once the centre of the Inca Empire and is rich in archaeological remains. The rainbow Inca flag still flies in the main square. We enjoy exploring this colourful city under hot sun and blue skies, and have time to reflect at leisure on our adventures – a relaxing end to a very full-on trip. We return to Lima so Cathy can catch her plane home. It is sad and strange to say goodbye, not knowing when or where we will meet again – made all the more poignant after spending a month together, almost twenty-four-seven. We exchange final waves as she disappears into departures, and I resolutely turn away, alone, to seek out the bus back to my hotel. With my friend Andrew's help, I survive Lima for several more days before my next flight, but I am glad to get away.

Peru has shown me the determination of human beings to adapt to contrasting and challenging natural environments. Lima is 12° south of the equator, on the coast, but only northeastern Peru, around the Amazon basin, experiences a typically tropical climate with regular rain and lush vegetation. Much of Peru is desert. The Andes experience significant rain, wind and snow, and wide daily temperature fluctuations. Andean people have been known to dwell at above 17,000 feet, where their bodies adapt to the altitude. Cusco, with its subtropical highland climate, is roasting, dry and clear-skied in July. Peruvians inhabit all of these areas, overcoming the various challenges of little water, extreme cold, searing heat and tropical humidity, all within one country. Impressive!

I confess to feeling deprived of some human comforts – always survivable, but the effects in Peru are cumulative. Outside the main cities, in tourist-standard hotels, there is often something which doesn't work: the hot water, the shower, the Wi-Fi, the heating. The air in small towns is polluted, and in downtown Lima the traffic fumes are, without exaggeration, suffocating. And after my 'full-on' tour in a challenging country, I now crave relaxation. I have the impression that, unless you are rich, life in Peru can be spartan, and that most people endure and make the best of routine challenges. The people seem tough, with determined expressions and not much laughter. In comparison, I feel spoilt and lucky to live in relative luxury. But I remind myself not to judge Peru by my own norms. My culture and lifestyle of material comfort and consumer goods does not, in itself, bring happiness. I do not know what lies behind some of the apparently dour faces I see in Peru. I have spent over a month there, but apart from one family and two children at home in the Andes, I have met no one outside the tourist industry, so I feel I have barely scraped the surface.

RAPA NUI: A PEACEFUL BREAK

Well, I finally got there!

The journey to Rapa Nui, or Easter Island, is tedious and tiring. I land at Chile's Santiago Airport at midnight and retrieve my luggage, but I have no idea what to do next. There are no signs, there is nowhere to get information and I don't have the Spanish to enquire. Everything is closed, but I successfully buy a small bag of nuts from a vending machine, then stand around for a while, thinking the world has stopped and feeling helpless and confused in this almost-deserted and half-lit airport. I then recognise a small group of people who were on my flight from Lima, standing with worried expressions, so I approach them... 'Isla de Pascua, por favor?' Their nods and shrugs reassure me that I have found some fellow travellers who are equally confused. We hang around together, hoping something will happen.

Around 1:30 am a uniformed official appears at a barrier and two people wander over. When they appear to be receiving attention, I follow. I am told to fill in a police emigration document to be allowed to board the Easter Island plane. At 2 am, and with a document solely in Spanish, this is no easy task, but somehow I am allowed to proceed with my completed form and check my bag in again. In departures I nod off several times, but when I have donned one support sock for the five-hour flight, I manage to hear the boarding call. I lose the other support sock during the sudden exodus from the gate. There is time for some kip on the plane after completing yet another form – this time for entry to Easter Island. We arrive at Hanga Roa, the only town, in bright morning sunshine and walk across to the tiny terminal hut, which I guess is probably the only one in the world with a thatched roof. No one asks for the Easter Island entry form, but I queue wearily and endlessly to pay US$80 for a permit to view the famous Moai statues. By this time most people, and all the taxis, have left. So I stand outside the building, digging out the address of my B&B and wondering what to do next. A dilapidated taxi eventually arrives, and the driver has no difficulty finding my accommodation – which, I am relieved to find, is fairly comfortable. The first thing I do is catch up on some sleep.

Relaxation, 'downtime' and a mistake

It's easy to relax on Rapa Nui, an affluent, tropical island which on first impressions seems rather tatty. It has a similar (anything goes) feel to Denman Island in Canada, semi-wild horses that graze anywhere, lots of large, sleepy dogs and a generally warm climate. Hanga Roa, the small town, is green and lush, and busy with many quirky, individually owned, tourism-based businesses, boutiques and eating places. My time there allows me some much-needed relaxation after the challenge of Peru. On four of my five days I take it easy. The Moai statues are the essential attraction, so I book a day trip to the main sites. There is an otherworldly atmosphere around the statues, and their history is well researched and documented. It is interesting to hear from our guide about his strong loyalty to Polynesian culture, even though the island is now governed by Chile. I allow myself plenty of downtime to wander and explore the area around Hanga Roa and am fascinated by a crowded cemetery where jostling gravestones, some of them joyfully outlandish to my eyes, speak of both Catholic and Polynesian beliefs. Another day I climb a small, extinct volcano for a view over the island and find a place to get my hair cut.

My mistake on Rapa Nui is to miscalculate the weather. I hire a bike and, on a fine August morning, set out on a rolling, twenty-mile circular trip. I have completely forgotten that it is the depth of their winter – duh! When I am farthest from 'home', the clouds roll in, a wind starts up, and the rain arrives – and I realise I'm not carrying my waterproof. The temperature drops, and I have never been so cold and wet on a bike! All I can do is struggle home in my shorts, shirt and down gilet, which gets soaked. The road is never-ending, the chilling rain is horizontal and my bum hurts more with each turn of the pedals, but giving up isn't an option, so onward I slog. I eventually arrive, exhausted and in need of a hot shower, back at my room. What an idiot to go without my waterproof!

My enduring impression of Rapa Nui is the sunset. On a clear evening I walk from my room to the island's west coast, where several Moai statues line up by the ocean. It is akin to a pilgrimage – many people are doing the same, some carrying picnic hampers and folding chairs. I find myself a suitable spot and sit for an hour in a gentle breeze as the sun drops into the Pacific, silhouetting the Moai statues against a red and gold sky. A magical moment indeed!

Because of its remoteness, I have been expecting Rapa Nui to lack luxury and sophistication, but how wrong I am! Although it is a small island over 2,000 miles from Chile, enterprising people have created a low-key, pleasant, Spanish-style tourist resort where I can relax in comfort. Latin and Polynesian cultures seem to coexist happily, creating an atmosphere unique to this distant island. Again, I am reminded to abandon preconceptions.

FRENCH POLYNESIA

It surprises me to find an EU immigration channel at the airport in Tahiti, and from that point onward I have to keep reminding myself that this is not France... is it? The Polynesian element has somehow been mislaid, and the French influence is remarkable despite its geographical distance of almost 10,000 miles. Papeete is a hot, sweaty port where one day is enough for me.

From bad to worse!

I take a ferry to a smaller island, Moorea. This marks the start of a period when I simply want the time to pass. I might at some point view the whole episode with some amusement and enjoy telling the tale – much like the perverse enjoyment of describing the package holiday from hell. But right now I need to summon my self-preservation instinct, determination and self-sufficiency to survive my time on Moorea.

I am met from the boat by my chatty B&B host who drives me, in a car that has seen better days, to my five nights' accommodation – but it isn't far. My room is in a garden annex with a small bathroom in a shed next door. The first thing I notice is the bedsheets, made from red, fleecy polyester – hmm, unusual! (I later discover that this can deter bedbugs.) I decide to go for a walk before eating but am delayed because the window will not close properly. My landlady can't see why I want to lock up, but she obligingly produces a nail file and uses it on the catch to make the window close. I am invited to use the kitchen in her house to prepare my evening meal, which I do in the presence of two pit bull-type dogs – large, affectionate, ageing, heftily fat females. As long as their owner is present, it feels OK to have them around. Before we say goodnight she points out the 'superior' bicycle I've rented from her. The darkness makes it impossible to look at it properly, but I'm not optimistic and decide to check it in the morning. She then tells me she has to go to work the next day, and that I am welcome to use all the facilities in her absence. I go to bed early, looking forward to checking my messages and writing my blog. Sadly, neither Wi-Fi nor data will work in my room. I begin to wonder whether I've chosen the right place to stay – things are not looking good!

The next morning I awake needing a wee, so bleary-eyed and in my nightshirt I open my door to go to the bathroom. There is no sign of my landlady, but the two rotund pit bulls immediately charge across the garden to greet me, and one delightedly rams her nose where I'd rather she hadn't. Barely awake, I am shocked and scared. I consider my plight while I'm on the toilet, now fully alert. With their owner absent, I dare not trust these two dogs, however friendly they might appear. I don't want to spend the day locked in the loo so decide to dress, pack my daysack, eat a quick breakfast and leave by bike as quickly as possible. Luckily the dogs have disappeared when I emerge. The bike, it transpires, is too rusty to adjust and therefore unrideable, so I leave on foot, walking along the coast road where I hope to find alternative accommodation. I ring my landlady and, explaining my problem in the best French I can muster, ask her to ensure that the dogs are absent on my return. She reluctantly agrees but can't understand why.

I walk for hours on a warm day and enjoy coastal views of palm trees and a silvery-blue ocean, behind which are steep and rugged, tree-clad mountains. The first hotel I try is full, but after several increasingly wearying miles, at the second one, which looks less pricey, I am shown a self-contained bungalow. The gardens are verdant with palms and flowering shrubs, and there is somewhere to swim. It's cheap for French Polynesia – a mere £132 per night, room only! (My landlady on Tahiti has told me that for local people it is cheaper to holiday in Japan than in French Polynesia. Her hospitality and kindness, in the comfort of Fare D'hôtes Tutehau in Papeete, prove to be the saving grace of my time in Tahiti.) I delay my decision about the hotel and start the long trudge back towards my accommodation. Passing a cocktail bar at lunchtime, I console myself with a margarita (well, two actually) and order a salad. I consider my mistrust of the pit bulls and the malfunctioning Wi-Fi and realise that without a decent bike I am stuck in a residential backwater. So I find, online, the hotel I've visited and make a reservation for three nights. I have to return for my luggage, so I decide to stay put for one more night, trusting my host to make suitable arrangements for the dogs. The second night passes without incident and my host, who seems concerned for her reputation, drives me to my new accommodation. Chatting idly in the car, she suggests to me that her B&B is perhaps more suited to younger clientèle…! Having to rely on the lift, this affronted and elderly woman decides not to comment and on arrival we part with a stiffly polite 'merci' and 'bonne journée'. I obtain a refund on the B&B, minus admin fees. Before going to bed in my new hotel room, I notice some itchy, red lumps around my ankles. Fleas? Bedbugs? Who knows – but irritating souvenirs of several disconcerting and uneasy days!

Stuck in paradise

To see Moorea properly, I would need a car, but I lack confidence with a left-hand drive so decide against it. On some level, too, I have had enough of French Polynesia and have little energy for the tourist trail. I feel uninspired at the thought of occupying myself for three days before returning to Tahiti. I choose not to swim and sunbathe because the wimp in me finds the ocean cold, and the current around the hotel is strong. Other beaches are privately owned. With not enough to do and days to wait before I can leave, I confess I feel lonely and imprisoned. But there could be far worse prisons than this, so I decide to find comfort in the blue skies and balmy weather. For my remaining time on Moorea I summon my patience and walk, read, shop and dine – and at least I can get online.

Moorea's saving grace is its claim to be the world's pineapple capital. I take a long walk to buy two from a roadside stall – sweet, soft and delicious – unbeatable! I buy salad, which I keep in the fridge in my room, and make lavish concoctions. And I find a roadside caravan serving cheap steak and chips. So the time edges by and I shouldn't complain. After Moorea I have two further nights booked on Tahiti, and I count the days to my departure. Can't win 'em all!

My lasting and saddening impression, from both Tahiti and Moorea, is of the style of colonialism. I have seen hardly any acknowledgement that these beautiful islands are Polynesian. A privately run taxi trip round Tahiti includes a visit to an unsigned ancient Polynesian site of worship; I otherwise find no hint of the Indigenous culture. There is a small museum but it is closed. Tahiti seems to be little more than a very expensive Département of France. I am also saddened by the economic contrast I see between the luxury enjoyed by typically wealthy tourists – many from cruise ships – and the much lower standard of living of Polynesian people. I acknowledge that my lasting perceptions of French Polynesia have been formed during a short visit to only two islands. I can only guess what I might find, had I the opportunity to visit for longer and to travel more extensively throughout the area.

THE COOK ISLANDS: A LITTLE PARADISE!

A very different Polynesia

Immediately on arrival at Rarotonga, the biggest Cook Island, I sense the relaxed atmosphere. The friendly hospitality I receive there affirms my peace of mind. Stu, one of my B&B hosts, picks me up from the airport. He and Lynn run the Te Manga Retreat and treat me like a friend. Rarotonga's capital, Avarua, is a low-rise, slow-moving, small town which I have a day to explore before getting a plane to Aitutaki, another Cook Island about 124 miles away. Tomorrow is Sunday and Lynn suggests I might find the church service interesting. Respectability demands that I wear a skirt, but I do not own one – so Lynn lends me one of hers. Imagine that, from a B&B host! The service has a strong Anglican influence and everyone joins in with 'Holy, Holy, Holy'. Some of the young people stand up to make public declarations about their commitment to Jesus. It is a colourful spectacle; from the guests' balcony I look down on a sea of teenage girls wearing bright yellow straw hats with upturned brims. The congregation sings lustily, raising the roof with heart and soul in competition with the loudly amplified, karaoke-style accompaniment. This enthusiastic worship is followed by a huge lunch to which everyone is invited, and I chat to some local people. It is a joyful and welcoming event, made all the more special because I had no idea I would even be there.

Adventures in Aitutaki

The next day I fly to Aitutaki, and what a welcome I receive at the airport! The owner of my accommodation meets me and bestows around my neck a fragrant garland (or lei) of frangipani. It's true! I have become a film extra in *South Pacific*! I have paid through the proverbial nose to rent his bungalow, and from the speed he drives, he seems keen to get me there. On arriving I am delighted – the bungalow is on stilts, self-contained with a balcony facing the beach and the sunset, and offers everything I need for a comfortable week's stay.

On most days I choose relaxing activities. I rent a bike and take a trip round the coast to find palm-fringed beaches, fallen coconuts by the hundred littering the ground, banana plantations and some very wealthy homes. Every passing local person greets me with

'Kiaorana' and a big smile, which, as a lone traveller, I find touching. I book a lagoon trip during which I swim from some idyllic beaches and visit One Foot Island, romantically dreaming of being marooned there with a very special person.

Back on Aitutaki, the only accessible eatery is a roadside food wagon with plastic furniture on a wooden platform. On most days I indulge in their delicious sashimi – a massive, raw tuna steak served with rice. I need only to smile to get chatting with fellow diners, so I linger on these occasions for longer than intended. One of these chance meetings leads to the most exotic birthday of my life, when I break all my dad's rules about motorbikes. I cherish the moments. Enjoying Māori song and dance live under a starry sky in balmy weather and with feelings of solid friendship, I can hardly believe my luck.

Another day the Māori king of New Zealand makes a state visit to Aitutaki, to mark the close affiliation of the countries. Seemingly everyone on the island congregates in and around a huge marquee to listen to speeches and enjoy Māori song and dance performances. After this a buffet banquet is served on long trestle tables. At the signal to start, the tables are besieged by grasping crowds. Cutlery is in short supply, so eager hands scoop potato salad and other delicacies, from large bowls. After about fifteen minutes, only empty dishes remain, fingers are well-licked, and some of the assembled folks can be seen vanishing into the distance with trays of chicken legs... Well, the food is free and provided by the state!

I have one unsatisfactory experience on Aitutaki: a whale-watching trip which I buy myself as a birthday treat. Only one firm is operating, so there is no choice, and they pay no heed to the whales' welfare. Out in the ocean, the boat pulsates to heavy rock music at high volume. We can swim from the boat; I try it but only once, as I find the current and the Pacific swell too strong and feel cold when I am back on the boat. I am saddened when, on spotting a whale, everyone is encouraged to dive in and swim towards it; environmentalists strongly advise against that. At one point our small boat comes directly alongside a humpback whale. I am not sure how safe we are at this moment, but it is a privilege to be so unbelievably close to this huge, apparently docile animal. Yes, we have seen whales, but at what risks to us and to them?

Resting on Rarotonga

Back on Rarotonga I have time to explore more fully. In Avarua the Māori influence is obvious. Though an independent country since 1965, the Cook Islands are affiliated with New Zealand for foreign policy, and the islanders have both New Zealand and Cook Islands citizenship. It is refreshing to find that the original Māori culture of the Cook Islands is respected and celebrated everywhere.

Roosters and hens have the run of public spaces, so birds scavenge unhindered around outdoor restaurant tables. I have just finished a leisurely lunch and am relaxing with a coffee when, from nowhere, a fully grown hen lands, with a loud squawk, on my empty lunch plate. I don't know whether to laugh or scream, so I do both! The eatery is aptly named the Lucky Rooster.

I sign up for a guided hike across the island with Pa, a quirky, locally famous Māori naturalist. The walk is quite challenging and towards the end we have to abseil a short distance down a bank, then wade across a stream. So surprised am I at my newly discovered abseiling skills that I slip and fall in the stream. My clothes get soaked (very pleasant on a hot day), but more importantly, my mobile is submerged in the water... potentially catastrophic! It contains all my photos and masses of information and documents I need for my travels. Back at Te Manga, Lynn gives me some rice to cover my mobile overnight and, with luck, absorb any moisture. To my relief there is no damage.

I have a few days to relax before Stu finally takes me back to the airport for my flight to Sydney, rounding off a wonderful twelve days. I have enjoyed the Cook Islands because of our common language, English, the easy pace of life and the presence of both western and Polynesian culture. It has been easy to obtain information and to make friends informally. I have heard about several events by word of mouth (including the church service and the best time to find fresh food at the local shop), and having friendly contacts on both Rarotonga and Aitutaki has allowed me to learn about the islands from local people. This is the first time since leaving the USA that I have felt truly 'at home' – while on some of the world's remotest islands – and I am reminded how generous and welcoming people can be.

AUSTRALIA – WOW!

When I arrive in Australia I am not expecting the excitement I feel – which at times is accompanied by disbelief. I am deeply aware of its physical distance from the UK while also knowing it is home to some of my family and my friend Janine, so reaching Australia has become a goal. I have wanted to get a feel for the distance, and I have certainly achieved this after my long, multistage journey from the UK. Uluru has always held a magical significance for me and I am fascinated by Aboriginal culture. Yet I know I am arriving somewhere with a history of British settlement and a culture which is predominantly Western. I am surprised at the mix of emotions which emerges for me.

It is dark when Anita meets me at Sydney Airport and drives me to a friend's apartment. How good to feel welcomed by someone familiar; during the past month I have spent a lot of time alone. The next morning, the view from my bedroom window shows me skyscrapers and office blocks, a typical urban landscape in stark contrast to the tropical, low-rise community I've just left. I do the first of many double-takes to be sure this is real, and have my first taste of the amazement I will repeatedly find in Oz. I have really arrived in this place I have so often wondered about. I am actually here and am looking out on Australian office blocks! This surreal sense of disbelief and thrill hits me several times on my first day while walking the coast from Coogee to Bondi Beach. Almost five months after leaving the UK, it gradually sinks in that I have arrived here. My amazement continues the next day in the centre of Sydney. I really do see the ibis strolling freely in the Botanic Gardens. The iconic images I have absorbed of the Harbour Bridge and Opera House are no longer a dream. I am stunned by the view of the coastline from the rotating platform at the top of the Sydney Tower, and do yet another reality check when I catch sight of Botany Bay, where British convicts landed in tough conditions all those years ago. The excitement still isn't over. In the evening, Anita takes me to the Sydney Opera House and treats me to *West Side Story*. Not only have I seen this fantastic piece of architecture, I have been inside and enjoyed an event it was designed for. Our final day in Sydney is more gentle – and I think I am tired from yesterday's adrenaline highs. We take a boat from Sydney Harbour, a huge and bustling ferry terminal, to Manly Island and have a relaxing walk along the coast.

The Red Centre

I still have difficulty explaining how I find Australia so surprisingly captivating. I am struck dumb many times on the next leg of my travels, in the Red Centre. The changing landscape below me, viewed from the plane to Alice Springs, is different from anything I have seen, filling me with curiosity and wonder. I join a four-wheel-drive tour of all the main Red Centre landmarks, staying in fixed tents on sandy campsites. The sand gets everywhere, invading my pockets and my holdall. The drysacks I have packed come into their own when I need to find clothes quickly in the cool of the desert night, and they find an additional purpose: protecting my stuff from the ubiquitous sand. We visit Uluru, where I begin to appreciate, with awe, its enormous spiritual significance to the Aboriginal people. That feeling of amazement hits me again when we celebrate, with some bubbly, a distant view of that huge rock as the sun goes down.

On our final night, we bivvy at Oak Valley Camp. I feel honoured to spend over two hours in the presence of Loy, an Aboriginal woman with a passion for her environment and history. She is one of the few to have benefited from an Australian education, enabling her to speak confidently about her life's work: to educate about the Aboriginal people so that their wisdom is understood and their culture is kept alive. For more than two hours she has me engrossed and awed by her accounts of history, ecology, diet, social traditions, hunting and gathering, gender roles, politics, regional differences and more. We follow her on a sweltering bushwalk, when she shows us the physical evidence which substantiates some of the ancient stories. It has taken us a long, bumpy drive to reach Oak Valley, but the rewards of bivvying for the first time and meeting Loy exceed all my expectations.

Over five days we have motored endlessly along unchanging red dirt roads to reach the key features of the Red Centre. Mesmerised by the passing scenery, my mind turns to reflect on my experience thus far. This is the result:

AUSTRALIA... THE EDGE?

So how to know this Edge?

Befriend it? Edge of what?

And maybe, in a parallel world,

Believe that I might touch it?

Come here, Dingo – watch me while I stand strong

With heavy, barbed, protective wooden stick.

Look me, defiantly and directly, in the eye

And I will whisper 'Steady, boy, steady...'

We will pass by, each in a separate world,

No longer strangers, but never to be friends.

Come closer, Kanga, let me see your scars

And feel your power – your idiot boundfulness

And I will sit astride your sturdy back

And fly with you abound the reddened earth

And we will share the joy!

And will I come to know the Edge of Wild?

Now face me, doubts, and let's stand square and tall

And we will share a mutual respect

That spells, in full, the course of no return,

The threat of sameness, spectre of disillusion,

Can I grasp this challenge, no rough-hewn stone unturned?

And will I come to know the Edge of Fear?

Now fledge yourself, my restless, tiny bird,

And unearthed, uninhibited, fly free,

Inspiring me toward a life 'as if'.

And I will be the dream, as well as live it...

And will I come to know the Edge of Crazy?

Come here, elusive dare, submerge me in the now,

That I be heart, not head

And have not care nor conscience.

Then I, forgetting discipline and bindings,

Will shout out my liberty!

And will I come to know the Edge of Sane?

Get over here, you jovial, crazy Aussies

And let us share our joy in this wide space

And crack our corny jokes with ready laughter

Touching each other's hearts before we part

And I will warm with momentary connection

–

And will I know the fleeting Edge of Love?

Now lay me down 'neath purple, cloudless sky

And let me dream Uluru's lost beginning

And watch the sun sink, slow, below the plain

And feel the ancient presence of Wanambi.

And I will see the limitless unseen

And will I know the far Edge of Infinity?

And, perhaps, with time enriched and mind unfettered,

The nature of this Edge might be revealed

And leave no trace of the enigma,

Of tantalizing wonder, of temptation

Of this unfathomably...

Unpredictably...

Unconsciously...

Unheard...

Unseen...

Unknown...

PS What did the wallaby say to the kangaroo?

I wallaby like you when I grow up!

Hospitality and drought in
New South Wales

Back in New South Wales, Anita takes me on a road trip. I am overjoyed to see my first kangaroos not far from our motel at dusk. To my eye they are such ungainly and ridiculous animals! After a hike in the Wurrambungles (what a lovely name for a mountainous area!), we head to Coonamble in the outback, where her brother, David, has a large farm. In 2019 they have had no rain for three years, and every living thing is drought-ravaged. Having seen the farm in easier times, Anita is distressed at the sight of the bare, brown earth and dying trees. The drought has forced David to sell many sheep, as he hasn't been able to cultivate their feed, and the few that remain drink from a small groundwater pool. It is a sorry sight, and the first time I have ever witnessed the destructive effects of drought and understood that accompanying feeling of helplessness.

In the outback I also learn the true meaning of flies. They are small, like British houseflies, but a veritable plague outdoors. I usually cover my head and shoulders with a net, but on the day I forget to pack it, they swarm around and give me no peace, constantly seeking out my eyes and nose for fluid. The local people seem to be used to them, but to me they are the biggest nuisance I have encountered to date.

In late September 2019 I stay with Anita in Katoomba, one of the main towns in the Blue Mountains. She generously offers me her large and comfortable rentable apartment. She introduces me to her friends, takes me out with her Bush Lemons hiking group and invites me along to a fire-planning meeting, where I begin to understand the true danger of bushfires. All the local people are aware that the Blue Mountains are vulnerable, and Anita meets with her friends so they can agree how they would support each other in case of fire. They circulate leaflets carrying advice on bushfire safety and discuss means of warning each other if fire approaches, and how they would rescue each other's pets if any of their owners were away from home. The advice that surprises me the most is that if they become trapped it is safest to stay in a secure place indoors – and one or two of the women speak of terrifying occasions when they have done just that and allowed the flames, the smoke and the heat to pass through.

December 2019 brings some devastating bushfires throughout Australia. I speak to Anita later to find that she has survived the fires OK but has welcomed friends, dogs and a cat to stay with her in Katoomba over Christmas when they were evacuated for safety from a major fire in the nearby Blackheath area. They have been tense and worried over the whole period. Tourism in the area, including lettings of Anita's apartment, has suffered badly, though by February it is beginning to recover. One of Anita's favourite walks is no longer possible because the landscape has been devastated. All of this brings home to me the fragility of their environment and the danger they confront annually.

Diverse environments

Australia is BIG! And therefore very diverse. I enjoy exploring North Queensland, then the Northern Rivers area of New South Wales – both very different from each other and from the Blue Mountains. From Cairns I take a day trip to the Daintree River and am fascinated by the exotic, rare plants, leaves and textures of the tropical rainforest, which poses for photos with flagrant vanity! This is the only time I eat kangaroo, which tastes beefy but is rather tough. To see the Great Barrier Reef, I take a boat trip. We visit the Saxon and Hastings parts of the outer reef, which in 2019 are still thriving despite environmental challenges. The wind is cold and the currents strong, and I am suddenly summoned back towards the boat because I am 'drifting' – but I manage a brief snorkel, looking down on some very lovely, colourful coral and beautiful fish.

At the Gold Coast Airport I am again reminded of Australia's challenging environment. We land through a haze from a not-so-distant bushfire; is it the sunset or the smoke that causes the darkening sky? I have booked a hire car for the next ten days. Fully-comp insurance is exorbitant, so I opt for third-party. The hidden price of that is the additional stress from driving even more carefully than usual to avoid an accident. The car is brand new, automatic (mine's manual), bigger than mine and has every electronic gadget, but I am tired so decide to manage without deciphering the satnav. It's enough to learn to handle this very different car. I am headed towards Mudgeeraba (rhymes with budgerigar) to stay with my Servas host. Oh dear! I underestimate the distance I will need to drive along the Pacific Highway and take the wrong exit, then get lost in the dark on small roads amidst impatient commuter traffic, constantly switching the headlights between dip and beam – nightmare of a drive. Eventually my host drives out to meet me so I can follow her. It is good to arrive with both the car and myself intact, and we spend a relaxed evening getting acquainted over a meal.

Gradually getting used to the car, I meander at leisure through the Northern Rivers area enjoying some stunning coastal scenery and exploring remote rural areas. The jacaranda trees, exploding into purple-blue blossom, are almost psychedelic as they welcome me to Grafton. My Servas hosts tend to live 'away from it all', and I have fun locating them. I find one couple after taking a small ferry to a quiet village on the Clarence River. Kaya and Reinhard live at the end of a winding, unmetalled track at the top of a mountain where they built their own home. They introduce me to the taste of black sapote (a fruit which tastes like chocolate sponge pudding), and we sing in harmony after a delicious macrobiotic lunch.

Joanne, my friend Barbara's sister, lives on a smallholding near Ballina where she and her partner are building a new home. I sleep in their caravan and hear about their anti-fracking campaign and a range of environmental issues. I have an unpredictable and happy time in the Northern Rivers area, staying with fascinating people, and I am grateful for their kindness.

Happy reunions

I go on to visit friends and family, which gives me a welcome break from the tourist trail – or at least from having to organise everything for myself. I am grateful when others plan the day, and I'm happy to stop travelling for a while, put my feet up and enjoy some relaxing company. The strong contrast between staying for several days with the same people in one place and moving on frequently makes me realise how superficial my impressions of many places en route have been, and what a demanding itinerary I have created.

After a gap of four years, it is good to see Janine – catching up, drinking gallons of coffee, chatting face to face and wandering along idyllic beaches – after relying on email and the occasional video call. Our mutual attraction is still strong and we have time to consider what possibilities might be open to us. It is good to spend time in the places she has described, and with her family, so that they become real to me. We explore more of the coast north of Sydney, then spend time in her neighbourhood, and I learn about the rhythm of her life. We plan to meet twice more, later in my travels. Our times together allow us to ponder about the future, but the opportunities are limited. We get no experience of consolidated time together, so we're unable to find out what it would feel like to live our own ordinary lives in close proximity. This is not the only time I question whether my whole itinerary is too fast-moving for any deeper connections to develop.

Meeting my Australian family, many of whom live in the Adelaide area, is a joyful experience and provides some surprises. My second cousin once removed, Liz, has been very kind and helpful in organising my accommodation with family members, so I am looking forward to meeting them all. My great-aunt and her husband, who emigrated in the 1950s, were brought up as low-church Protestants, with a strict, teetotal lifestyle. I am half expecting the old religious traditions from two generations back to have been maintained – and to need to watch my Ps and Qs...

Walking up the slope at Adelaide Airport, I hear someone call my name. I look up and am surprised and delighted to see four grinning women leaning on a barrier, which they have draped with an Australian flag. All second cousins once removed, they are Liz, Brenda, Diane and Mary – and I begin the challenge of piecing together my Aussie family tree. Back at Brenda's in Glenelg, we chat over (lots of) bubbly, and I have the time to appreciate my warm welcome to Adelaide. I gladly drop any remaining worries about historic, stringent religious principles, and I soon discover that I am part of a large extended family who love a reason for a get-together. One of these is held at Mary's in Seaview Downs. There are over twenty of us spanning four generations. It is a fun afternoon, but it is, and still remains, hard to keep track of all their names and relationships. What strikes me is that after my time in Adelaide I will be leaving with plenty still to discover. From two Lancashire émigrés has developed a huge network extending from Adelaide to Tasmania to Perth. I can only hope, in the time available, to get to know a small corner of this huge family. I am also struck by the difference between my large Adelaide family and my own, very small one in England. Large family gatherings are a new experience for me. When three of these take place in Adelaide, I am happily and noisily entertained to the point of exhaustion, and I appreciate the opportunity to get to know them all and witness their apparently easy and relaxed relationships. But the available time allows me only superficial impressions, and I come away curious to know more about the dynamics and undercurrents of this huge network.

Liz and her husband Bob take me to Clare, where we stay with more rellies. It is an unmissable opportunity to look at vineyards and experience (in full!) the winemaking culture. We continue towards Liz and Bob's home about three hours north of Clare, across vast wheat-growing areas with huge silos, and through small towns, some of which are dying as a result of people moving away. Laura, a quiet, tree-lined town, is the home of the Giant Twin, a high-quality choc-ice – kept in business, it seems, by Liz and Bob! Bob drives us across seemingly endless, flat agricultural land and, via Port Augusta, to their home in Whyalla.

Whyalla is a steel-making town of about 24,000 people on the western coast of the Spencer Gulf. Despite (or perhaps because of) the remoteness, there is a sense of community. It is easy to see the difference between the modern steel industry in Australia, with its valuable contribution to the economy, and England's industrial heritage. Whyalla's blast furnace opened in 1940, and the buildings and associated housing are tastefully laid out in typical, spacious Australian style. Extraction of iron ore takes place at a huge, expansive mine located near the town of Iron Knob. The iron ore here is noted for its high quality. There is none of the depressed feel of the older British steel towns with small, terraced houses crowded around slagheaps.

Getting to know the south

Mary meets me back in Adelaide and we take a two-day trip to Kangaroo Island, off one of the southernmost points of the Australian mainland. I find its beaches even more beautiful than those on the mainland, if that is possible. The island is home to seals, koalas, penguins and many other seabirds, and offers spectacular coastal scenery including Remarkable Rocks, which more than live up to their name. I am delighted when the seals on the beach lollop across to greet us with friendly curiosity. After a day of fresh air, we come across what looks like a typical English tea room with tables and chairs laid out on a lawn. The very pleasant surprise is that they specialise in gin – so we conveniently forget we had been looking forward to a pot of tea and allow ourselves an indulgent evening. I am sad to hear later that Kangaroo Island has been devastated by bushfires, and that the wildlife has seriously suffered. This news is upsetting and even more difficult to digest after two days enjoying this island's wild beauty.

In Tasmania my friend Sue books us a trip to Maria Island. The whole of this small island is a nature reserve, and visits are carefully regulated, so going there is a special treat. There are no cars and we use a handcart to take our bags from the landing stage to the bunkhouse, the only accommodation on the island. Known as The Penitentiary, it used to be a prison and its façade is suitably plain. Exploring the island, I am again awed by the coastal scenery and delighted to be able to walk very close to wombats – rather like cute, huge hamsters. I stroke one, only to be totally ignored; the wombat is more interested in sniffing out food. The Tasmanian devil is found only in Tasmania, and its numbers have fallen because of disease, so sightings are rare. Naturalists have taken some healthy specimens to Maria Island and encouraged them to breed, and numbers have been slowly increasing – so I am delighted to spot one in the distance.

Back in Hobart I seek out Liz's son Tony and his husband Carl. We enjoy a luxurious, long weekend with excellent food and wine, taken for walks by their exuberant and affectionate boxer, Louie. I take a bus ride to Hobart's historic 'Female Factory' where female convicts from the UK were housed on arriving. Some of them had been deported for minor crimes such as petty theft. It is a bleak reminder of some very harsh living conditions and the frequent cruelty often inflicted on the women. They made their living by offering a laundry service and by picking oakum until their hands were raw. I am lucky enough to attend a lunchtime concert in Hobart by the world-famous ensemble Van Diemen's Band – another happy reunion with baroque music.

Melbourne, which I grow to like, is the only place that appeals to me as a place to settle. My friend Sue generously opens her home to me, sharing her life and friends for over three weeks. I have time to explore independently and get a feel for the place. 'Messy Melbourne' is my affectionate term for it. It's not a beautiful city, but it seems to offer all the benefits of London and has some of the 'red-brick' feel of Manchester – the two cities I know best – so I feel at home. I spend a lot of time on user-friendly commuter trains, I meet a local musician who can potentially introduce me to others, I find the street with all the outdoor gear shops and – oh, wow! – I fall in love with Korean food! Sue and her friends take me on a four-day trip along the spectacular Great Ocean Road, where we see yet more stunning coastal scenery and I have my only sighting of a koala, which is asleep in a tree. We go to exhibitions in and around Melbourne and explore other parts of the coast. The special highlight is the Women's T20 Cricket final, seen by a crowd of 85,000 at the huge Melbourne Cricket Ground – and Australia soundly beat India. It is high-powered, noisy showbiz – a huge contrast to what we quiet Brits would expect at the Oval.

Impressions of Australia

I love Australia. It is more stunningly beautiful and diverse than I'd ever imagined. I have experienced the most amazing environments, especially the Red Centre, which inspired me to write a poem. The big skies with expansive views to infinity, warm breeze and beautiful sunsets around Adelaide are second to none. Every bit of the coast, it seems, has the most beautiful beaches. Something about Australia enables me to feel unpressured and liberated. Outside the cities there is room for everything to spread: homes (many large bungalows), the land attached, the wide roads and the distant horizons. It's nothing to drive 250 miles because the traffic is sparse, the pace is easy and the cars are mainly automatic. Amongst whites I have seen no hint of the class distinction so prevalent in the UK. Aussies tell it like it is, swear if they want to, call each other 'mate' and have unpretentious place names such as Iron Knob.

I have met Aboriginal people firsthand and learned not nearly enough about their history and their balanced and respectful relationship with the land. Their wisdom makes so much sense, but there is little room for it in modern Australia's juggernaut approach to some aspects of the environment (extractive industries, pipelines and coal seam gas). As with many Indigenous populations, Aboriginal people have been disrespected and misunderstood for generations. Modern economic systems will not accommodate their naturally adapted lifestyles. Despite some efforts to help the Aboriginal people and the 'First World' settlers to integrate, there remain many seemingly insurmountable issues. It's no surprise that racism still seems to be deeply ingrained in some white Australians.

Nowhere is perfect, but something has touched me deeply in this far-off place. Had I visited forty years ago, I might have been tempted to stay for good.

NEW ZEALAND – AND RAIN

North Island

While Australia exceeded my expectations, I am sadly underwhelmed by most of New Zealand. The weather is hindering me, along with a lingering chest infection which saps my energy. I'm finding New Zealand an interesting country and meeting very kind people, but I see little of its reputed scenic beauty because of rain, low cloud and poor visibility.

Despite feeling weakened by my cough, I find the energy to attend a joyful Christmas concert at Auckland's modern and spacious Holy Trinity Cathedral. The performance is truly uplifting and reminds me how much I love, and am missing, hearing good, live music.

My next memorable experience is a visit to Waitangi, where I learn about some of New Zealand's attitudes to Indigenous people. The 1840 Treaty of Waitangi ostensibly established unity between the British and the Māori. The signatures of many Māori chiefs were obtained, alongside British dignitaries. But the Māori didn't know that their version of the treaty had linguistic discrepancies, which meant that their status under the treaty was diminished. This has caused tension ever since, and though some Māori rights are guaranteed, there is a constant worry that the treaty could be revised to reduce their rights. I am glad to see that Waitangi is a national monument, with Māori exhibits and cultural shows, and is respected by people of all backgrounds.

My coach trip on a fine day, from Rotorua to two major geothermal sites, is amazing. As the area sits on the join of the Pacific and Indo-Australian tectonic plates, the earth's crust is thin, and escaping gases give the whole place a sulphurous odour. The last local eruption was in 1886, and there appears to be no concern about further instability – perhaps because there are so many geothermal vents to release pressure. I spend the day wandering close to gloopy bubbling mud pools, waterfalls, and pools which are brightly-coloured (lime-green, turquoise, yellow, pink and more!) from mineral deposits. We see a geyser which always erupts at 11 am and wonder at its meticulous punctuality – only to learn that this is engineered by pouring soap solution into its outlet, lowering the surface tension. But the teasing worked at first! We all take a boat trip to see geysers genuinely erupting sky-high with water and steam, and volcanic craters. It is a unique landscape not to be missed.

Napier was rebuilt in Art Deco style after a major earthquake in 1931. On another fine day I take countless photos of this town centre's rich architectural heritage, a huge number of attractive and well-preserved buildings. At a community art gallery I almost buy a beautiful and symbolic painting by a Māori woman but decide against it at the time. Several days later I find myself chatting to a self-professed art expert on a bus. He is cantankerous and reeks of alcohol but he intrigues me. Janine is with me and can barely contain a warning scream at my (apparently) naïve level of trust when I hand him my mobile to show him a photo of the painting. He advises me to buy it... so, I do. I arrange for it to be shipped to the UK, in case I return there, and plan to hang it wherever I decide to live. A happy souvenir of a fine day in Napier!

South Island

My one enduring experience of New Zealand's stunning natural beauty is my self-guided, 35-mile, four-day hike, in glorious sunshine, along the Abel Tasman Trail in the north of South Island. It's an easy walk on well-maintained paths and very well-signed, so I can relax, unchallenged, to the rhythm of my footsteps and the sounds of nature. The ever-changing beaches and inlets, tree ferns and other vibrant greenery, and deep blue skies grace me with beautiful views around every headland, and I have never heard cicadas so loud! After falling in a stream in the Cook Islands, I am proud of myself when I manage to judge the tide and wade successfully, barefoot and knee-deep, for a hundred yards across an inlet. Each time I stop to eat my packed lunch I am vigilant because scavenging weka – the cheeky, flightless birds common in this area – are brave enough to steal any unattended food. One morning after a boat ride from my accommodation to the start of my day's walk, I am wandering along a wild beach lined by tree ferns and scattered with dead trees. My phone rings. It is Mary, one of my Adelaide cousins. She very sadly tells me that her daughter, whom I have met, has died unexpectedly during surgery. Words of condolence feel hollow considering this huge shock and tragic loss for Mary, which is shared by the whole family. It is a sobering jolt for me, and I sit down for a while on a log to take stock until I am again ready to amble along in the sunshine. When I see Mary again, back in Adelaide, I am struck by her immense strength and resilience.

A highlight of my New Zealand experience, in Little Kaiteriteri, lifts my spirits. Although I was enthralled by the scenery of the Tasman Path, since arriving on South Island, I have spent a week with very little conversation – brief and casual when it does occur – so I am feeling lonely. This morning, under another clear, blue sky, I have left my stuff in a hostel and am enjoying a walk over a wooded headland, listening to a new kind of birdsong. One particular song is so perfectly tuned that I use the tuner app on my phone to discover that the bird has chosen the key of A major – so I join in with some harmony. I am looking forward to finding the chalet in Little Kaiteriteri where, by coincidence, Liz (my longtime soulmate and fellow Gozo traveller) and her friend Mary are holidaying. When I arrive, the chalet is locked and all is quiet, so I wander down to the beach. It is a joyful and surreal moment when two bathing beauties splash through the waves to emerge from the sea and come running across the beach to greet me. We share some happy hours together and laugh a lot while Liz and Mary teach me to play Qwirkle, and we eat in a good restaurant with a view out to sea. Liz and I enthuse about the Pohutukawa tree, known as the New Zealand Christmas tree because of its bright red flowers, which are at their best this time of year. Liz and Mary have rented a car, so the following day we go for a long drive and explore at leisure the northern tip of South Island. Our itineraries then diverge, but we meet again briefly in rainy Queenstown, with more Qwirkle and some Thai food. I can't overstate how heartwarming and magical I find it to meet up with good friends in such distant places.

After organising several holidays with friends, I have earned a reputation as a travel planner. Living up to this, I make a humdinger of a plan to travel from Nelson in the north of South Island to Pancake Rocks at Punakaiki on the west coast, which come highly recommended. My perfect plan goes like this: taxi (4:45 am), plane to Christchurch, plane to Hokitika Airport, taxi to Hokitika Town, bus to Greymouth, bus to Punakaiki. It goes superbly, and I congratulate myself when I arrive at Hokitika Town after the second flight and taxi ride. I go to the visitors' centre to find a three-hour diversion before my bus departs, and speak to a very helpful assistant. She is in fact so helpful that she tells me I could have caught one bus direct from Nelson to Punakaiki. Suppressing a choking fit, I retreat hastily and beat myself up soundly – it had never crossed my mind that a bus might be the best option. Once I've recovered my composure and self-respect, I decide to make the best of Hokitika – after all, it is a very expensive added extra. I find some interesting driftwood installations on the beach and some shops selling jade ornaments and jewellery. I concede also that the views from my flights have been utterly awe-inspiring. I have flown (twice!) over the wild, mountainous interior of South Island. Some of the mountains are snow-capped, and most of the valleys appear unexplored (or at least uninhabited). Almost totally wild and empty!

I have a long southbound bus ride to Fox Glacier. The views might well be panoramic on other days, but today they are obliterated by low cloud and rain. The bus takes me over Hercules Hill on a road which, two months ago, was totally blocked by huge landslips during storms. I have never seen so much bare earth (there has not been time for plant growth on the reconstructed hillside) or wrecked vegetation, and I realise how powerful nature can be in these parts. I am also struck by the suddenness with which the hills rise steeply from a huge coastal plain – compelling evidence of ancient tectonic shift.

In southwest New Zealand I feel lonely and stranded for too long. I haven't been able to find any Servas hosts and have resorted to ten nights on the trot in hostels or B&Bs – and it has rained and rained! Safe and well-fed though I am, it is hard work to take all the conversational initiative, and the exchange of travel tales is beginning to pall. Adding in long periods under grey skies and café umbrellas waiting for the rain to stop, I have become very fidgety, consuming too much coffee and reading too much. Thank goodness I brought my tablet, which at least makes the reading easy. Outside the main towns, indoor activities are very limited, and the great outdoors is unwelcoming because I don't like getting soaked, even when I wear decent waterproofs. There is little I can do but dig in and be patient. It is like being stranded on the worst day in Elterwater – apparently at Fox Glacier it rains, on average, every other day.

It is the same when I reach Queenstown – sitting under café umbrellas to stay dry for what seems like days, with brief, light relief when I meet Liz and Mary again. On what turns out to be the only dry day, I hike up a steep trail to the top of Bob's Peak for some panoramic views across Lake Wakatipu and take the cable car down. Despite the weather I book a day trip to the famous Milford Sound, which is like a Norwegian fjord. After an early start and a very long coach ride, we board a boat for an underwhelming trip along Milford Sound, though I do see, through the rain, some pretty, ribbon-like waterfalls. A few days later – and thankfully after I left Milford Sound – the only access road is completely blocked by a landslip. Supplies are helicoptered in. Tourists are helicoptered out. So much of life on mountainous South Island, it seems, is at the mercy of the weather.

Tourism's highs and lows

More than nine months into my trip, in Queenstown in the rain, I have time to reflect. I am still enjoying the travelling and experiencing new places, and living out of my holdall has become quite a habit (what will I do with all that stuff in storage?). The tourism, however, has become more of a challenge – absorbing yet more views and information when I am beginning to feel satiated. But I have some appetising plans for the rest of my touristic time in New Zealand, and on my return to Australia my priority will be to get to know people. So I feel ready and willing to complete my year's travelling.

I decide on a group cycle trip which lasts several days along the Otago Rail Trail, followed by a scenic train ride to Dunedin. We cycle past sleepy villages which thrived during New Zealand's gold rush, and where architectural styles and shopfronts have been preserved. I feel transported back to those pioneering times. One or two villages have gastropubs, where we dine in the evenings.

In remote Naseby we go to a curling rink. Wearing non-slip shoes, we have a hilarious time learning how to remain upright while pushing a stone, and then polishing the ice to persuade the stone to skid a few more inches – an unexpected diversion!

I am tired of the tourist trail when I reach Dunedin, but my very hospitable Servas hosts look after me well and I am kind to myself, acknowledging my need to stop. When I reach Christchurch, my final stop in New Zealand in 2020, that 'tourismed-out' feeling remains – but Christchurch has to be seen because it was the epicentre of a huge earthquake in 2011. The gaping devastation of the old cathedral is a unique, unforgettable and heartrending spectacle which dominates the city centre. I am fascinated by the 'Quake City' museum, which offers detailed insight into the geology and human impact of several earthquakes, with helpful scientific background and videos of earthquake survivors describing some horrific times. I find especially touching a mother's story of how she was desperate, but unable, to find out whether her young son was safe in his school. Christchurch and its inhabitants were shattered by the events and are still recovering over ten years later.

Though my time in New Zealand has not been the best, I have had no real lows. At times I have felt lonely or stranded by the weather, but these periods have passed. I realise I must accept these challenges as part of travelling's ups and downs. What I also realise is that tourism can be tiring. After months of finding out for myself what attractions are available and organising my own visits, summoning the curiosity to absorb yet more stimuli and information is beginning to feel like hard work. I return to my question about the initial planning of my journey and wonder whether I would have been happier staying in one place for longer to get a better understanding of how it could be to live there. This will turn out to be one of my lingering questions about the whole experience, and one to which in retrospect, I would have given more thought beforehand.

GUILLOTINE!

In March 2020 I am in Melbourne for the second time, staying with Sue for three weeks. I am glad to have longer in Melbourne this time round. I want to find out whether I fancy several months in Melbourne during the UK winter, so I set about exploring – and I am acquiring a warm familiarity with both people and places. As March progresses, Melbourne's major venues begin to close down in response to a threat from a new virulent killer virus, and the Grand Prix is cancelled. Sue and I have tickets for a baroque music recital which is also cancelled, but the situation in Melbourne, and Australia in general, seems much less serious than in Europe. I learn from news broadcasts that Italy in particular is struggling with a heavy incidence of the infection. People are dying and hospitals cannot cope. News reports on TV are horrific. Alarm bells ring.

I have more plans to fulfil before my scheduled return to the UK: I am to stay with Sue in Melbourne for nine more days, getting more used to being there, enjoying the Melbourne Gay Film Festival and possibly meeting some local musicians. I'm appreciating her very welcoming set of friends and feeling generally at home. I have a flight to Sydney booked at the end of March, to spend a few days with Janine before leaving Australia. I have booked a week's small-group travel from Bangkok to Chiang Mai in northern Thailand, followed by a 'counselling retreat' in Chiang Mai, to prepare myself for returning – or not – to the UK. I am looking forward to being in a very different cultural environment as my final treat, and to distilling my thoughts about 'what next?' When I learn that Thailand has succumbed to this new virus, albeit not too seriously, I question whether it would be wise to go there, not wanting to be stranded in hospital in an unfamiliar country. So I phone everyone I can think of to get some opinions. This decision, however, is soon pre-empted.

On Sunday 15th March, I awake to the news that Spain is overwhelmed by the new virus and has closed its airports. This is a decisive moment. It seems very clear that it is only a matter of days before the UK follows suit (ha!), and I do not want to be stranded. Two hours later I have booked a flight from Melbourne to Manchester and cancelled my remaining plans. I will leave Melbourne late on Monday the 16th. This, I discover, is not a moment too soon. Owing to the Covid panic, the price of the same flight will have more than doubled just a few days later, leaving many people stranded.

This whole episode, with its rapid development, leaves me in shock. Abandoning my visit to Thailand is a huge letdown. Leaving Melbourne nine days early is a wrench. Cancelling my time with Janine before leaving Australia is painfully upsetting. Then the realisation hits me: THIS IS THE END OF MY TRIP! After travelling for eleven months, it feels as though a guillotine has fallen, heralding a huge and sudden change for which I am utterly unprepared. Add to that some uncertainty about the amount of contact I will have with Lancaster friends on arriving back, and the outlook is bleak. At the time I don't know whether anyone will meet me in Lancaster, but I know neither Cathy nor Helen is prepared to put me up in case I've caught Covid on the plane, so I book a room in Lancaster's very basic budget hotel. I find this upsetting but have to accept it, eventually coming to appreciate that they have little choice. I am tearful during my lift to the airport with Sue, hardly believing that my enormous journey is ending so unceremoniously, yet knowing I am to take my last flight. The airport is a desolate place, though still in operation.

My flight goes well and I get adequate sleep, arriving in Manchester around midday on 17th March. The airport is very quiet, but there are no additional checks on new arrivals, which surprises me. I stride through immigration, baggage reclaim and customs unimpeded. My train is eerily empty, but otherwise the journey back to Lancaster feels like putting on an old glove. My relief is palpable when I see Helen waiting on platform 3. She greets me warmly, though I sense some underlying apprehension. A big hug isn't allowed, so we touch elbows and she walks with me, socially distanced, to my hotel. She buys some food for me and leaves it outside my hotel room. I truly appreciate this kindness which, compromised though it has been by advice about Covid, helps me to feel welcomed. Sitting alone afterwards in yet another sparsely furnished room, and looking through the smeary window onto a grey, deserted street, life seems bleak. I steel myself for what will be, effectively, another week on the road. This is my 'welcome home' after eleven months away – not what I hoped for.

True to form, I manage to banish the disappointment and find a more optimistic viewpoint. I am safe and healthy (touch wood) with a place to sleep. Extending my time 'away' by an extra week, in this hotel, will do me no harm. Staying in a cheap hotel in Lancaster at the start of a pandemic is a new situation and a challenge I am ready to tackle. So the same day, I speak at length with several friends and arrange to meet – with due regard to the social distancing advice. I make plans for the rest of the week and go out for a walk. Then I sleep for eight hours and awake refreshed – ready for the next phase of my life and all set to start sorting things out: cello, bike, house rental, car. I believe I have been lucky to arrive back in the nick of time, with the unknown future of life in a pandemic before me.

SECTION 5: READJUSTMENT

After any big adventure or life-changing experience, there is always a need to readjust. This applies whatever you choose to do. My readjustment was not entirely about how to deal with returning to Lancaster; much about it was familiar, which meant I knew my way around and saw many familiar faces. The readjustment was more to do with my own attitudes, which had changed while I was away – and they still hadn't settled. Covid, of course, added complications. My readjustment was as much about feelings as it was about events.

SAME TOWN, VERY DIFFERENT CIRCUMSTANCES

One week before the UK's first Covid lockdown, it was hard to recognise the Lancaster I had left eleven months previously. On Easter Sunday 2019, Lancaster had been at its best: a sunny, vibrant town enlivened by buskers. People out for a stroll wore shorts, enjoying the weather and chance meetings with friends, and the shops, cafés and pubs were comfortably busy. Walking the same streets on my return – oh, what a difference! The grey skies didn't help. Word was out that we were at the start of a killer pandemic. As our final week before a possible lockdown progressed, I saw fewer and fewer pedestrians, and there was less and less traffic. I had never experienced this atmosphere of paramount uncertainty and discomfort. Perhaps this was what it was like for people living under a reign of terror with a possible threat to life round every corner. Covid was the 'Unknown Enemy' and as such had to be treated with the utmost caution. People in general were to be avoided.

Familiar faces could no longer be trusted. 'Stay at home!' was becoming the adopted mantra. Fear prevailed.

I had to find a means of coping with this new situation while preserving my sanity. I could not, and would not, let Covid prevent me from living my life, so I viewed it as a challenge and made some practical decisions. Lockdown was not yet decreed, so I would go out and about normally, distance myself well, avoid crowds and wear a mask in shops. In truth, having spent eleven months adjusting regularly to new situations, I was more intrigued than perturbed when I wondered what we were all in for.

With increasing warnings of a full lockdown, my priorities were clear – and urgent. I contacted the removal firm who were storing my stuff and hesitantly asked whether I could collect my two cellos and a bike. Would they be accessible, and how would I transport the cellos? Luckily the items were easy to locate, and the firm kindly delivered them to my hotel. Sharing my very small room with two cellos and a bike turned it into an obstacle course, and I bruised my shins on the pedals – but I now was happily reunited with my treasured possessions and could get about locally. I knew I would also need a car, to give me the freedom to travel beyond Lancaster, and I had very little time to find one. A local solution was needed, so I contacted dealers, looking for a safe, cheap car which would keep me on the road until I decided what to do next with my life. During the final weekend before lockdown, I cycled miles in fine weather to test drive several cars, and I enjoyed the exercise. But by the end of Saturday, I had burned many calories and found nothing I liked, and I suspected that some of the dealers had boosted their prices for this lone, older female. Feeling despondent, I had but one remaining option scheduled for Sunday morning: a longer bike ride to a garage I had previously dealt with. And luck was with me – I found the ideal car at the right price! With great relief I cycled to collect it on the first day of lockdown, and with the back seats down, it held my bike as I drove it back to Lancaster.

At the end of my bleak week in that shabby hotel room, Cathy was satisfied that I did not have Covid, so I was thankful to move into her spare room. It was a huge relief finally to stop travelling. But we were faced with a new situation which neither of us had predicted. The day lockdown was decreed, Cathy's kitchen had been ripped out – and under lockdown, fitting the new one was extremely slow. Her dining room housed the fridge-freezer and two electric rings. Groceries, crockery and utensils were kept in plastic crates on the floor (another obstacle course), and we washed up in the bath. Yet another challenge! But we adjusted to the new routine and soon discovered that sharing Cathy's home during lockdown was an ideal solution for both of us. We each had company rather than isolation. Taking turns with the cooking added variety, and we managed to work out how to share the space.

UNCERTAINTY REMAINS

Having arrived back in Lancaster prematurely, and with the limitations of lockdown, I found it difficult to consider my way forward in the long term. I was still struggling with some major questions:

- Is any kind of future possible for Janine and me?
- Do I want to remain in the UK?
- Do I want to make Lancaster my home?
- How can I find more fulfilment if I stay in Lancaster?

But I soon realised that, for the duration of lockdown, Lancaster was where I had to be. Other decisions could not be made at this point. So, I absorbed myself in practicalities: perusing the almost-dead property rental market, knitting Cathy a sweater, reading, discovering new local walks, editing my travel blog, watching TV and shopping for food. I also delivered prescriptions for a local pharmacy, which gave me a sense of purpose and was good exercise when the spring weather allowed me to cycle. Coincidentally, my windproof jacket was the institutional blue of the NHS, and many people waved and smiled as I cycled past. Someone even clapped! Lacking physical space and not wanting to disturb, I didn't play my cello. Cathy dealt with the continual challenges of contacting her kitchen supplier and organising life to accommodate workmen, and we maintained social distance by hanging a curtain between the living room and kitchen.

I am eternally grateful to Cathy for allowing me to stay, because I would otherwise have been homeless – even the hotels had closed! House rentals had almost come to a standstill, so I stayed with Cathy until the end of June 2020 – more than three months. We were both relieved to regain our own space when I finally moved out, but we agreed that our arrangement had provided a happy and mutually beneficial solution during the first lockdown.

Considering that we were in lockdown for much of this time, life was quite varied and satisfying. I eventually found a house to rent, only a short walk from Cathy and Jude and her partner Tracey, and moved in on 1st July, glad to finally have my own space but aware that this rental arrangement was only temporary.

THE SIGNIFICANCE OF 'HOME'

I had been in regular contact with Janine, but meeting again in the foreseeable future was impossible. We discussed various options, and I almost decided to spend six months a year in Australia once Covid travel restrictions were lifted. Ultimately, and very sadly, we had to abandon our plans. To make the best of living in the present in Lancaster (as I had no option) I needed to think of it as home, however temporarily. I found it impossible to combine this with any sense of Australia as home. The dream gradually disintegrated and the ambivalence and turmoil defeated me. Ditching our plans was painful for both Janine and me, and much was left, unhappily, unresolved.

As I write, several years later, I am glad we have retrieved the best of our friendship, and Janine continues to live happily in her established home in Australia. Overall, the experience provided me with an important discovery regarding the significance of home, after considering the various options of expat living. I now see that I need the security and stability of belonging wholly in one place. My hometown provides roots which are more important to my identity and peace of mind than I had realised.

Unpacking my stored stuff and settling into my newly rented home was enjoyable and time-consuming. I needed a few new bits of furniture, so Helen and I made an adventurous post-lockdown trip to IKEA, and when I wasn't assembling flat-packs I could enjoy playing my cello again. As the Covid restrictions began to lift, I spent more time out walking with friends, especially Jude and her dog, Freya, and enjoyed outdoor socialising in small groups. The world was gradually coming back to life.

Late in July 2020, I was hit by another realisation. To celebrate my new home, I decided to hold a small 'garden-warming' with shared food, and along came Cathy, Helen, Jude, Tracey and Jenny. We spread our contributions on the table indoors, taking turns to fill our plates and glasses, and seated ourselves at suitable social distance in the sunny garden. This was the first time since April 2019 that I had sat down in a small group with some of my closest and dearest friends – and I suddenly felt loved! Nothing I had experienced throughout my eleven months away could compare with the complete sense of belonging which enveloped me in that moment. I was almost overwhelmed by the emotion of my simple thought: 'These are my people!' After all my angst about where to settle, my question about Lancaster was answered. The next day I started house-hunting.

Reflecting now on that development, I can see why I decided to stay in Lancaster. Over my eleven months of travelling I had met countless kind and generous people – including my welcoming Australian family. I had wondered about a more extended stay in Melbourne, which felt like a potential home. I had even considered living part-time in Australia. Yet nowhere had I experienced anything approaching the warm, caring and relaxed familiarity of my close friends on the day of my garden-warming. I realised that, despite experiencing some wonderful time away, on some deeper level I had missed the presence of my close friends, and our strong, easy, mutual acceptance. No amount of searching the unknown – which I usually find exciting – could provide this very powerful sense of belonging. The decision about where to settle was not about analysing the benefits of different places or forming strong bonds with people who were new to me. It was the result of an emotional response: feeling loved. Again, I trusted my gut. I was also aware that the value of those strong friendships I had (and still have) in Lancaster was rooted in the years it had taken to build them. I did not relish the idea of starting that process again in a new place – it was one huge risk too many.

Deciding to stay in Lancaster was stabilising, but there were more questions to answer about how I would like to live my life. An old friend, Annie, amused me with her sayings. She was the first person I heard describe someone as 'mad as a box of frogs'. One of her maxims was 'Do what makes your heart sing!' This advice featured large in my future decisions, and I will always thank Annie for planting it in my mind.

So I allowed myself to dream. Music had a prominent place in those dreams, which soon became a vision and then a plan – and it crystallised like this:

I want a house where I can make music a central feature of my life, and invite people round to sing and play together without worrying about disturbing the neighbours. I want to live close to my friends, in the part of Lancaster I already know and like, and not far from the town centre.

Practicalities emerged from this vision: detached house with space for music, in the Fairfield or Abraham Heights area of Lancaster.

I had been viewing houses for six months and had no luck. The property market had still not fully recovered after lockdown, but prices had begun to rise. There was one house that appealed, but I thought it was too expensive, and believed I could find something cheaper and more suitable. I had the proceeds from my previous house sale available, and nothing to sell, so thinking I was in a strong position as a buyer, I decided to wait for the 'right' house. After three more months of finding nothing, I discovered that the house I had liked was back on the market. It needed work but ticked all the boxes, so I quickly made an offer, confident of my success. But... oh dear! The seller rejected my offer because her previous buyer was again able to proceed, subject to a successful sale of her existing property. It was a huge disappointment. I carried on the search, feeling wistful whenever I passed the *Sold STC* sign outside the one house I had wanted. Ho-hum. I consoled myself by building a hedgehog box in case one of them was house-hunting – and I was delighted in the autumn when it was adopted, providing the perfect home for a nephew of Mrs Tiggy-Winkle.

Life continued into the second lockdown and the Christmas and January of 2020–21. My friends and I had a WhatsApp group and one-on-one social bubbles (with occasional permutations which maintained the spirit of the restrictions). We broke the rules occasionally by meeting outdoors as a group of four. Just before

Christmas 2020, we met outside the back of Cathy's house and sang carols, washed down with soup, bread and mulled wine – a joyous, rebellious evening! (Little did we know about happenings in Downing Street.) It was Jenny's birthday in January, so we again dared to misbehave with reckless abandon. On a cold, grey morning we wore all our winter gear and sat round a trestle table outside the café in Lancaster's Williamson Park, with cake and hot drinks. It didn't take much to generate a festive spirit amidst lockdown restrictions in dismal weather.

House-hunting opportunities had almost ceased over the Christmas period, so I continued with my usual routines of carefully masked shopping expeditions, long walks or bike rides alone or with one person, cello playing and too much TV. Cathy and I spent Christmas together, and we both fell asleep in front of the telly just in time to miss the Queen at 3 pm. I was weary of the whole property scenario and had resigned myself to even longer as a tenant. One morning in January, I was enjoying the excitement of putting some pasta in a shopping trolley when my mobile rang. The name on my screen was the estate agent selling the house I had liked, but I could think of no current reason for her to phone me. 'Are you still looking for a house? It's just that the one you made an offer on has come back on the market again, so I wondered...' I didn't hear the rest of her sentence. When I 'came to' after questioning my senses, I managed to understand that the house I had wanted was again available to me. Joy and relief! This time my offer was accepted, and completion followed in just five weeks. Allowing time to make some major changes to my new house before moving in, I continued to rent for another two months. Luckily tradespeople were available to start work as the winter lockdown was now ending, and it became my enjoyable mission to organise a massive programme of home improvement. I moved into the house in April 2021.

UNENCUMBERED AFTER ALL THAT?

The feeling of encumbrance had figured so large in my developing plans that I had gone away with desperate hopes that this particular aspect of life would improve. Ideally the encumbrances would fade away, never to return. You may well be wondering how that went. Here is a brief description of the changes that occurred, using the list I started with.

Housequandary: The house in the wrong place, with a daunting garden, has been replaced. My new house is detached and an ideal size. It has a small, manageable garden and a music room. It is very close to Cathy, Jude and Tracey, and my back gate opens into a community orchard, which is my shortest route into town and idyllic with apple blossoms in May. I have gradually turned this house into a home that I love, where I feel happily settled, though before my travels I never truly believed this was possible. Not only that, I am happier in the neighbourhood surrounding my new home. Early in 2021, when tradespeople were starting work again, rules remained about how many people could share an indoor space. So, conversations with workmen took place outside the front of the house. This enabled people to get a good look at their new neighbour, and many of them welcomed me. In the street I got to know my opposite neighbour, Annik, quite well. Finding some common ground, especially regarding music, we began having coffee together. It didn't take long for us to discover the amazing coincidence that we'd been to the same school (forty-five miles away!) and that I'd sung in a small group with one of her brothers. Annik introduced me to her older sister, Michèle, whom I then also remembered from music at school. In short, this unlikely event was the start of a wonderful new chapter of music and friendship – and all because I moved to this particular house. How lucky!

Moggiemalady: I have no pets at the moment. As I go away often, my lifestyle lacks the constant routine needed by cats and dogs. I love animals, but as things stand, it's easier to make a fuss of other people's pets, and talk to farm animals over the hedge, rather than share my home with any four-legged creature. I occasionally visit Margaret and Cleo, who still remembers me. Sophie is sadly no longer with us, but she had a happy few years with Margaret. If and when I stop travelling, that could be a good time to offer an animal a home.

FOMO: Any fears of losing my social contacts were unfounded. No one I value has changed or moved away, and Covid has strengthened my closest friendships. Four of us started a WhatsApp group during the pandemic, and we have kept this going. It is now our first stop for organising any social events or celebrations, alongside the strong one-on-one friendships we already had. These Lancaster friends have become my surrogate family. My book group continues, and on my return it was easy simply to rejoin. The same is true of other pre-existing groups, and my new friendships in the music world are enriching. Thanks to Annik, my neighbour, my musical contacts have multiplied. I still play in several baroque ensembles with my great buddy, Jude – and now also with Michèle – which I love to do. Thanks to Annie's advice to 'do what makes your heart sing' I have also nurtured new musical circles. I joined the same choir as Annik and Michèle; this is exhilarating and fun, giving a different kind of satisfaction. Through attending residential baroque music workshops, I have an expanding group of friends from across the country. We sometimes organise our own get-togethers and enjoy playing in different settings.

Years ago I sang and played the guitar semi-professionally, and after a long break, I have picked up my guitar again. I now enjoy updating my repertoire of songs, learning new ones and even, occasionally, writing one. I am exploring local opportunities to sing and play, which introduces me to very different people in a world of non-classical music. As I had envisaged, music is central to my life, giving me untold joy and always offering a rewarding challenge and social life. In truth, I struggled for a while to keep up with too many new musical commitments, which was stressful. Now, after dropping two regular activities, I feel I have a better balance – and I do not feel as though I have missed out.

Cellomania: I still enjoy playing the cello, which now takes its place more comfortably amongst different musical activities. I frequently host chamber music sessions at home and experience great joy playing Handel and Corelli with friends. However, I travelled without a cello for eleven months. Being on the move and experiencing new people and places effectively displaced my obsession and proved to me that I can manage without a regular cello 'fix'. I was surprised that, on the few occasions when I felt the need to play, this passed, and I discovered the delight of writing my blog and the occasional poem. This pleasure has remained since my return to Lancaster, enabling me to write this book. As I am more emotionally detached from the cello,

I am free to do other things and have time for other musical pursuits.

Oldfogeyness: Ageing is inevitable, both in mind and body, but there is well-documented evidence that we can assert some control over its pace. I hope I have slowed my mental ageing since the start of my planning. Long-term travel forced me to tolerate – and survive – discomfort and occasional awkwardness. I had additional practice in handling situations which did not go according to plan. It is easy to absorb the subtle messages in our ageist culture, such as 'you need to be careful', 'don't take on too much', 'that's too heavy for you', 'don't overdo it at the gym', *'now you're getting older...'* and to cosset oneself unnecessarily in a cuddly world devoid of challenge or excitement. I hope I am learning to resist ageist assumptions and am more open to doing what I feel capable of, both physically and mentally. I confess to being more relaxed in my approach to physical exercise – it's fine to cycle shorter distances and enjoy easier walks. Looking at a high mountain horizon can be as satisfying as the view from the top. And I still go to the gym but don't exhaust myself. Stagnata is still there to help when a part of me needs to be on autopilot, but I am quicker to notice, on rarer occasions, when she tries to take over. I feel light-hearted about trying new things and more courageous about changing direction when something isn't working out. I hope I am discerning enough to know when to say 'yes' or 'no', though I still prefer 'why not?' to 'why?' Living in a smaller house, in a friendly neighbourhood, I am more confident that all will be well if I leave the house unoccupied. Going away itself has become easier because I now have a standard checklist of all the necessary small jobs to do and items to pack – so it is easy to be thorough without stress. I have no doubt that my journey has made a positive difference to all these aspects of mindset.

The 50% club: I went away prepared to be flexible about my orientation. In fact, it was never challenged. Almost always I found referring to it unnecessary, except very rarely when I encountered heterosexual assumptions – usually expressed by an inappropriate choice of pronoun, which I corrected if necessary. To everyone I met, my orientation appeared unimportant. I enjoyed the company of most people regardless of their gender and resolved, from then on, to be more open to friendships with men. After my return I am very happy with my lesbian lifestyle and my identity is unchanged, but my social circles are more varied than before I travelled. I still value and appreciate my lesbian friends but have plenty room for others, so life is enriched.

Overall, I am careful to keep a check on the balance of my life, and if I sense that something could become an encumbrance, I try to change it. I am wholehearted about the things I do. And I hope and believe that, with increasing years, I'll become more discerning in my choices. I am wary of complacency, so I try not to take anything for granted, but I have been on a fascinating journey and reached – for now – a much happier place.

THE JOURNEY CONTINUES...

After almost four years back in the UK, I have had time to reflect on my experiences. Some of my thoughts are not what I expected.

Memories

My resounding recollection is of the kindness I received almost everywhere. Never in my life have I so consistently, and for such a prolonged period, experienced such warmth, hospitality and genuine care from strangers, friends and family. In most cases my relationships were superficial and fleeting (this happens when travelling – a rolling stone gathers no moss), but I had wonderful company when I needed it, without which I could not have done what I did. I remain grateful to all those who gave me their time and energy.

To revisit any of my experiences?

Some of my experiences were so enjoyable that I want to repeat them. My wonderful musical experience and the friends I made on Denman Island beckon me back. Since the pandemic, Andrew and Robert have resumed their Denman Baroque project and organised a performance of an opera by Lully in May 2024. I was seriously tempted! Before my travels, I expected my visit to my family in Australia would be a one-off. But I remember my exact feelings when I left Adelaide after my second visit: I was certain that I would return. Now, I am not so sure. Regarding both of these experiences, I have a cautionary inner voice which tells me, 'Never go back.' I fear that to return could spoil some of the magical memories. Could I possibly find the same level of enjoyment this time round? And if not, might I be disappointed? As I write, these answers elude me.

Staying in touch

Since my return, I have done my best to stay in occasional touch with everyone who was so kind to me, whether by email, video call, WhatsApp or Christmas cards. I have wanted to show my appreciation, and I am keen to hear more about their lives and well-being. As it is, I remain in touch with only four people, though there are others with whom I know I could reopen contact. I have needed to find an explanation for this lack of communication, to help me avoid a feeling of rejection, and what occurs to me is this: I think and hope most people took in my appreciation the first time I expressed it, and they have no need for repetition. In Servas, people come and go; that's just the way it is, no expectations. And for a busy person, keeping in touch for the sake of it can be a burden. So, I accept that we all continue with our self-contained lives unless there is need to reconnect. And that's OK.

The itinerary – did I get it right?

At the very start, I had hoped to spend longer in some places, to gain some depth of experience. In reality I planned an itinerary that did not allow this. I had not truly considered the balance between breadth and depth, and I unwittingly chose breadth, with brief visits to many places. Looking back, I now realise that to have both breadth and depth over only one year's travelling is impossible. There were times when I travelled too quickly to take it all in, and my time with new friends was too brief to allow any deeper connections to develop. Continually moving on meant I spent too much time receiving kindnesses and not enough time giving back. But I am content with what I did – because we can never know what might have been. Looking back on all the places I visited, there is none where I would now want an extended stay unless my visit was for a specific reason. But I do know I could have planned it all very differently, and who knows how it might have turned out!

Timing

People ask me whether, at age 66, it was the right time to take an adult gap year. Might I have achieved more earlier in life, with a younger person's energy? Did my ageing mindset limit me, causing me to lack a sense of adventure and take too few risks? I hope my answer to these questions applies to everyone: *every individual knows when the time is right.* One has to feel ready, and this cannot be forced. Maybe it's because action is problem solving; things happen once there is a significant issue which cannot be ignored. Yes, my age limited me sometimes. I swam only once on each boat trip so that I could dry off and avoid feeling cold. Not fancying the rigours of the Routeburn Track, I opted for the easiest self-guided walk in New Zealand – and had an idyllic few days! On many evenings I stayed in my room for peace and quiet, so I might have missed out on some interesting conversations in the hostel kitchen. The choices I made suited me at my time of life. I was not ready any earlier, and I am glad I left it no later. If I had been younger when I travelled, the rewards would very likely have been different, but whether better or worse, we cannot know.

Did I develop personally?

I am sometimes asked whether I developed any inner resources. I think the answer to this must be yes, because I am happier now than before I left. I think I have developed more self-sufficiency – essential for anyone travelling alone. Before my travels, I quickly resorted to contacting others if I was at a loose end. Now I find I often choose to be alone, quietly and uncompromisingly pleasing myself. I have discovered the fascination of writing: searching for the words that express exactly what I mean. I think I am more adaptable, accepting whatever reality arises and trying to make the best of it. I believe strongly that it is impossible to know for certain what will bring joy or happiness, because that involves prediction. However thought-through our decisions, the unplanned and unintended can bring special moments. Learning this has been liberating because I now have less need of an agenda and I love spontaneous rewards. It took me over a year and a trip round the world to make complete sense of 'You take yourself with you wherever you go'. I took myself travelling in 2019 and brought back an almost identical self in 2020, but my restless spirit has, for now, settled, because the most precious thing I have discovered is acceptance and love of the present moment.

Have I changed?

I have asked myself whether I have changed as a result of my year away. Yes and no. I am almost the same as the person who left in April 2019: musical, energetic, analytical, opportunistic, irreverent, bonkers, and I hope friendly, sincere and kind. I went away prepared (hoping?) for a major revelation concerning the direction my life would take, but there was none. Surprisingly, the pandemic was the pivotal event of my whole year because it caused me to return to the UK. Without it, boarding my final flight as scheduled, from Thailand to the UK, might have felt like a cop-out – to return 'home' rather than choose somewhere else. But I could accept the need to return to a secure place, with all my personal attributes and baggage, because of the pandemic. It was the Covid pandemic that brought me home.

One positive change has been my decision to help at a food bank. I am angry that, in this wealthy country, there are people who cannot afford to feed themselves. Viewing that in contrast to the kindnesses I received on my travels, I decided to try and give something back in Lancaster. So one day a week I volunteer, stacking shelves, dragging heavy trolleys and preparing food parcels. It's fun and totally different from anything I have ever done. My colleagues are a friendly bunch, and the physical exertion of lifting and carrying heavy loads helps to keep me fit. I return home exhausted and am glad to relax.

I still travel, but without that underlying question about 'home'. Lancaster, and the life I am developing here, are what I feel I need. So my travels consist of one-off trips, usually to warmer places in the winter months. (But having been caught in snowdrifts and a blizzard in Morocco's Atlas Mountains, I now know that even winter warmth cannot be taken for granted.)

At the time I arrived back I had no idea how or whether my journey had made a difference to my life. Now, I am certain it did. I am more at home than I have ever felt. I have come to appreciate what the here and now of life offers me, and the old, discontented, restless spirit has, at least for the time being, settled. No amount of spiritual development, therapy, introspection or analysis could have made this difference. I had to go round the world and return at the start of a pandemic to discover what really matters. Paulo Coelho's illuminating and readable book *The Alchemist* offers a similar perspective.

THE HERE AND NOW

My journey began with the resolution I made, at the age of 65, not to 'wake up at 75 and wonder where the last ten years have gone'. This resolution opened the gate to my 'positive ageing' adventure. Now, at 71, the adventure is not over – though it has calmed down – and I do not want it to end. I am enjoying my 70s and the enthusiasm with which I approach each day. I cannot be certain of anything as time passes, and I have no wish for certainty – which for me would lack excitement and challenge. But what I do have is the fundamental belief that every day is a gift and how I live it is up to me – not only in what I do but in the attitude I bring to every situation, new or old. Life still presents some specific challenges, and I accept that I have to handle them – nothing is ever perfect. But I have, for the foreseeable future, decided that Lancaster is the place for me, and I have invested time, energy and money in my home.

I am more able than I was before my journey to count my blessings and find ways of accepting and handling the challenges. It is often helpful to remind myself of the Buddhist emphasis on impermanence: everything changes. This includes the good things and the bad. Ageing is here to stay, but I hope the learning I have achieved through my journey will enable me to sustain a positive approach. I also hope that you, dear reader, will feel it has been worthwhile to stay with me this far. If this book has helped you clarify anything to assist your way forward, then I am happy.

POSTSCRIPT:
SOME SUGGESTIONS FOR
A POSITIVE EXPERIENCE

It is important for me to emphasise that these can only be suggestions. I offer you a digest of the things that worked or didn't work for me. And I invite you to disagree; most of these ideas are debatable.

Things happen when they're ready to – but keep the door open.

I spent several years feeling somewhat lost and directionless. All my self-questioning did no good, until something happened to jolt me into action: a chest infection. I was surprised how the ensuing events fell into place and led me to sell my house and go travelling.

A similar event led me back to Lancaster. I had no clear idea about where to go after my eleven months away. It was the pandemic that caused me to decide to return.

'Keeping the door open' for me meant allowing things to happen and being open to change, requiring a state of mind that had no clear sense of direction. This meant I had to accept that nothing would happen if I clung to my present lifestyle and habits. I remember cutting out a tiny piece of advice from a newspaper: 'If you always do what you've always done, you'll always get what you've always got' (attributed to Henry Ford).

Embrace serendipity and find the spontaneous opportunities.

Life happens – whether or not we plan it. But if we leave the door open to opportunity, there is a greater likelihood that serendipity will pay a visit. Many unplanned events, even the undesirable, contain the seeds of opportunity. My illness provided the starting block for my whole project. The chain of events went like this:

- Chest infection
- Thinking about spending winter outside the UK
- My love affair with Gozo
- Realising Gozo wasn't for me, though my outlook had broadened
- Listening to conversations

- Exploring possibilities
- Distilling the life-changing plan

Conversations, and listening to underlying messages which are unwittingly dropped into the mix, are crucial. Several unplanned exchanges – and especially my friend's use of the word 'encumbered' – were turning points in my life. Telling people spontaneously about my plans brought unsolicited offers to introduce me to friends in distant locations – and this sometimes led to places to stay and new friendships.

Take notice of powerful experiences.

My resolution on my 65th birthday not to look back at 75 and wonder where the last ten years had gone was a feeling I could not ignore. It opened me to more radical possibilities than I had previously considered, and this new state of mind helped me move forward.

I had been very determined to explore moving to Manchester and had expended cartloads of energy in planning it, and house-hunting. I had thrown myself into this despite a few underlying doubts because I believe the only way to find out if I'm on the right track is to have a wholehearted try at it. I was bitterly disappointed when I finally realised, deep down, it just didn't feel right. But I am glad I decided to find out.

Manage risk head-on and question 'rules'.

Everything we do involves risk of some kind; things might not go according to plan. Even when we carry out routine tasks, we do so based on calculated risk and previous experience. I am glad I decided to calculate risk and not to avoid it, because it enabled me to enjoy new experiences.

Risk management required me to stay alert, to heed my internal safety gauge and follow its advice. I also tried to take any necessary precautions (and failed when I left money in my room in a hostel, allowing someone to steal my dollars!). These safety concerns absorb energy, and it was harder for me to sustain them when I was tired. So my underlying recommendations for a safe and happy experience are to recognise your energy levels and avoid planning too much, along with making sure you get enough rest.

Questioning rules applies especially to those we bring with us from childhood. My dad's rule about motorbikes was still with me in my late 60s, but I finally decided to ditch it and do what was normal in the Cook Islands – where the motor scooter, without a crash helmet, is the common form of transport. I calculated the risk, decided to trust my new friends, and had one of the best evenings of my life.

'Don't accept lifts with strangers.' For me, French Polynesia did not offer a good experience. If I had accepted a lift with the well-dressed French woman on Moorea, who knows where this might have led? I am glad I kept this rule and refused the lift for my safety, but I accept that I will never know what might have happened – for better or worse.

Both Janine and I took some risks to find our way forward. After some joyful, and some very challenging, times we have set a course which is comfortable for us both. Without the exploration, I (and I think both of us) would have lived with the regret of wondering what might have been possible.

Face the difficult questions, especially about yourself.

I mean questions about what you do, what you believe and how you see yourself. This was the most challenging part of my planning. The honest answers I found to some of my questions, and especially regarding my encumbrances, were often hard to accept. The encumbrances I unearthed, by writing them down in a list, all brought difficult questions about how I lived my life – and even who I was. But I could not have begun to make changes to my life without confronting them.

It was tempting to run away from my question 'How important is my lesbian identity?' but I allowed it to remain in my mind, and it gradually became less scary and more approachable. The same fear arose when I recognised Stagnata and the need to change some of my attitudes. I found it helped not to dismiss the uncomfortable questions too quickly. By allowing a small space for those questions to mull, the discomfort soon diminished and I could face them head-on.

As older women, many of us feel guilty or frightened at ideas which look like 'abandoning our responsibilities', but if we allow ideas to linger, negative feelings can often change and soften. This is empowering, enabling us to consider the important questions without panic or avoidance. Helping ourselves to self-question, without judgement, is also an important reason to have strong support.

Slow down!

This was especially important and challenging for me because I see time as very important and like to save it. Hence, I have a deeply ingrained habit of doing routine things as fast as possible. Attempts to change this have been interesting but not always successful. Sometimes I recognise the need to start to slow down but then forget and speed up again. Stagnata allows me to carry out routine tasks quickly with little or no thought – so I continue to struggle with simply slowing down.

Yet on the rare occasions when I have achieved a slower pace, I have found the space to celebrate some rewards. I stood still in a forest on Hornby Island after some rain and opened my senses. I allowed myself the time to jot a few things down. With time on my hands that evening, alone in a B&B, I invited my creativity in and the result was my poem 'Forest'. Being marooned in the rain in Queenstown, and again in Cromwell, New Zealand, forced me to reflect on my travels and how they were affecting me. I had time to admit that I was becoming weary of the tourist trail and needed to prioritise my plans. I began to accept that I could take it easy in some places, with more time to rest. Travelling was, for me, about finding a balance between moving myself to a new destination and simply staying still and experiencing the place I was in at the time. If I were to plan the trip over again, I would give myself more time to stay still.

Expressing this in more general terms, I have come to believe that after a major change of any kind, it is important to give the new circumstances enough time to settle, and to remain in that new situation long enough to reach the best possible understanding of its advantages and disadvantages. This can take longer than first expected.

Change can be tailored to fit.

FOMO (Fear of Missing Out): Taking oneself away from a situation often raises insecurities about what we might miss – that amazing 70th party that someone has planned, the perfect purchase after many years of searching, the changes we might have to adjust to on returning, and the fear that we might no longer fit in. I had all those fears but (with some difficulty) I set them aside. I had to analyse my fears and decide which, if any, really mattered. It soon became clear that missing the 70th party and the ideal purchase would make no long-term difference. It's true that I have lost some people from my life, and from a new perspective have decided, myself, not to pursue some historical 'friendships'. But I have gained others, chosen with greater maturity in later life, and find new delight in them. Removing myself from my original situation enabled me to view life from a new perspective and tailor it accordingly. Yes, on my return, I had to adjust to some new circumstances – and this continues – but the overall picture is more satisfying and dynamic than before my travels.

Be flexible and try to say yes.

I was glad I sought a balance between 'broad-brush' and detailed planning. The broad brush helped me to keep an overview of my journey without pinning down too much detail. I knew when I was due to arrive in and leave each country, but planning in more detail depended on circumstances. I felt the need to organise my accommodation in advance, but wherever possible I booked with the option to cancel. When I reached a destination I usually had no detailed plan so I could simply allow time to unfold. This approach gave me the flexibility to say 'yes' to appealing ideas and invitations (the Vancouver seaplane, the Nazca Lines in Peru, Chaco Canyon in New Mexico, the Grouse Grind near Vancouver and my wonderful birthday on Aitutaki). It was also important to allow myself to do very little if I chose. And as my energy for touristic activities waned later in my travels, I was glad of this flexibility. Flexibility meant I could change my plan if necessary – as I did when a chest infection sapped my energy in New Zealand, and when I chose to move accommodation on Moorea. Of course, the biggest change of all was my early return to the UK – and I am glad I decided on that.

Reflecting now, I still question the balance I found. I realise that with even more research and planning I could have squeezed more out of my time in many places – but at the cost of spontaneity and energy. I cannot know what might have been! And it would be kidding myself to cling to the notion that all my plans were perfect!

ACKNOWLEDGEMENTS

THANKS TO LOCAL FRIENDS

My experience would have been much more challenging – nay, impossible – without Cathy's help. Specifically, she opened her home to me when I needed accommodation both before and after my travels. She willingly received parcels of things I no longer needed and gave them storage space. She allowed me to use her address for mail, and she kept a full record of all my accommodation details en route, in case of concern or emergency. She stayed in touch with me throughout. All of these actions gave me the peace of mind to plan my journey thoroughly and to enjoy it without excessive worry.

I offer my heartfelt thanks to my local friends Helen, Jude, Tracey, Jenny and Philippa, for their patience, inspiration and support before and during my adventure, and since I have returned. Their willingness to engage with me over the planning helped me to be confident that there was little I had omitted.

Friends in my book group helped me to mark the start of my physical adventure by hosting a shared lunch; this added to my confidence that this was a place to which I could return.

I have great appreciation for all the people who responded to my blog despite the platform's user-unfriendliness. Their responses, and the conversation snippets arising, helped me to understand that they were interested and cared.

I thank all the people mentioned in my 'Serendipity, Not Anonymity!' section for helping me to find company.

I am grateful to my friends Jill D, Cathy P, Joan E, Sue J, Dorothy P, Gill D, Liz B, Tracey K, Helen J and Helen P for conversations, inspiration and feedback during the development of this book, and to Roger Grant and Bonnie Craig for some helpful suggestions regarding publication.

THANKS FOR KINDNESS EN ROUTE

Dinah from Vancouver, for meeting me after my first flight, showing me Vancouver, giving me accommodation and introducing me to Chrissy, whom I later arranged to meet on Gabriola Island. Dinah and I climbed the Grouse Grind together – an utterly humbling and very steep slog to the top of a mountain overlooking the city.

Anne and Rick, Denman Island. They gave me accommodation, hospitality and friendship during the Denman Baroque project and after my trip to Hornby Island. Nothing was too much trouble. They showed me round, introduced me to many fascinating local people and organised the loan of a bike. Janey Bennet from Washington State was also staying there and introduced me to her friend Judith from Hornby Island when she came to our *Fairy-Queen* performance.

Andrew, for the loan of his cello and for meeting me from the chain ferry to Denman Island. Originally English, he is one of the organisers of Denman Baroque.

Judith Lawrence, a published writer from Hornby Island, for a wonderful meal and evening of conversation.

Judith lives in an isolated house, farms her own land and is a respected local environmentalist.

Wanda on Gabriola Island. We got chatting on a beach, and she took me out in the afternoon to see some ancient petroglyphs and a massive redwood tree.

Chrissy from Vancouver and her friends on Gabriola, with whom I went to a dance and shared some delicious food.

Kerry in Albuquerque, who gave me a bed for an amazing ten days and shared her Buddhist life and friends, including Jeane, who also showed me the local area. Kerry showed me Chaco Canyon – a real taste of the Wild West! She drove me to my Servas host in Santa Fe.

Marianne and Kim in Santa Fe, for a half-day hike on the Aspen Vista Trail and a delicious lunch, Christmas-style – which means you get both red and green chili sauce!

Lynn and Stu, who run the Te Manga Retreat in Rarotonga in the Cook Islands, for their welcoming kindness and sharing their home, making them much more than just B&B hosts. They took me out for an afternoon on their semi-submersible boat. While staying with them I shared the breakfast table with three women attending an international conference for Jehovah's Witnesses. This was my first proper conversation with JW people. They were wonderfully kind and interesting.

Anita in Katoomba, for all her friendship, generosity and support in Australia – and for staying in touch!

Joanne and Bruce, near Ballina, who put me up in their caravan while they were building their new home.

Glenn and Joy, who showed me and Janine the old town of Dungog near Sydney.

Jacqui, in Hobart, who is the niece of Barbara (Gozo) and Joanne. We met for lunch and she told me about her work. She looks after pademelon wallabies, possums, wombats, Tasmanian devils and other mammals and birds who have suffered in the wild. She is utterly dedicated, finding it hard to say 'no' when an animal is suffering.

Sue, friend of my walking friend Jean, who showed me many new places (Maria Island off Tasmania, the Great Ocean Road) and shared her Melbourne home with me for over three weeks. Her wonderful photos greatly enhanced my blog!

Dottie and Gwenda, friends of my Kendal friend Helen P, who live near Tauranga. Dottie gave me a comfortable place to stay when I was still fighting off my chest infection.

Jim and Ian in Wellington, friends of Pam in Manchester. We had a fascinating day together, and they showed me the nature reserve Zealandia, reached by a funicular railway. We met again for coffee on my last day in Wellington.

Trish, the daughter of Elaine, my cellist and bass-playing friend. At the time, Trish was very active in community music and theatre in Nelson but has since moved away. We went out for a meal, enjoyed getting to know each other and discovered we shared many views about music-making.

My friends Liz and Mary for lovely company in Little Kaiteriteri and Queenstown, and for taking me in their hire car to see the northern tip of South Island.

Aart and Leigh in Dunedin. Aart lent me a cello and we played Vivaldi together, him on bass viol, while Leigh cooked us a delicious meal.

Angela and Marlene, who took me to a Bauhaus exhibition near Melbourne. Angela for the loan of her bike and for taking me to the National Gallery of Victoria.

THANKS TO 18 SERVAS HOSTS

(I cannot guarantee that the information presented is up to date, nor that the people who showed me such kindness are still involved with Servas. The facts were accurate in 2019–20.)

I received warm and welcoming hospitality in the following places:

Oak Bay, Vancouver Island: a wonderful introduction to the Servas experience and a fabulous blues guitar recital.

Nanaimo, Vancouver Island: a celebrant with a strong interest in personal development and who has set up a public library in a glass-fronted cupboard outside her house.

Gabriola Island: a retired folk singer with a great sense of humour! The host's home is called Chelm. (In Jewish folklore, the inhabitants of this Polish town, Chelm, think themselves wise, but stories tell of them coming up with dumb solutions!)

Issaquah, near Seattle: a marketing consultant and a teacher, who gave me a lot of insight into the local economy and fabulous hospitality.

Inner Richmond, San Francisco: a trauma psychotherapist – and we laughed!

Day hosts from Flagstaff: outdoor enthusiasts who have walked the 800-mile Arizona Trail and now help to maintain it. They took me out for the day, then for breakfast, and helped me find my Greyhound bus.

Santa Fe, New Mexico: my bookbinder friend who had travelled overland to India with her two children. She went out of her way to help me and made wonderful chocolate crunchies for me to take to Peru.

Lima: a Peruvian-Italian woman who spent a day showing me round Lima and introduced me to the buses and taxis which the local people use.

Mudgeeraba on the western edge of the Gold Coast conurbation: my host had lived in Germany and travelled extensively, especially in the US.

Crabbes Creek, Northern Rivers on a remote hillside, in a house they designed themselves: my hosts left Germany in 1995 and travelled in a camper van for a year before settling at Crabbes Creek. We sang together one day after lunch.

Lawrence, on the Clarence River: a well-travelled couple, now doing creative work with textiles and volunteering at their local history museum.

Auckland, New Zealand: a retired linguistics lecturer and a political scientist. I stayed twice with them, and we met again in Taupo from where they drove me to Napier. They were supportive friends for my whole time in New Zealand.

Haruru near Paihia, North Island: a nurse and a market gardener. They offered me many helpful suggestions about New Zealand.

Coromandel, North Island: a singer who plays recorder and was active in developing the local Steiner School. Her husband is a keen environmentalist. They have cycle-toured in many countries.

Thames, North Island: One of my hosts originally came from Chichester. They have travelled widely and lived in France. We had a great rapport and chatted and laughed late into the evening, and they drove me to my next destination over two hours away.

Musselburgh, Dunedin: they showed me round and were full of interesting conversation. An expert in lilac plants and travels widely, giving talks.

Day hosts in Dunedin: took me to Tunnel Beach, a stunning small sandstone cove, and showed me the Otago peninsula.

Christchurch, South Island: a psychiatric social worker and a ward manager in a local hospital. They have both travelled widely and supported surgical crews in Palestine.

FURTHER READING

Applewhite, Ashton. (2019) *This Chair Rocks: A Manifesto Against Ageism*. New York: Celadon Books.

Clear, James. (2018) *Atomic Habits*. New York: Random House.

Coelho, Paulo. (1993) *The Alchemist*. New York: HarperCollins.

Daniels, Siobhan. (2022) *Retirement Rebel*. Sheffield: Vertebrate Publishing.

Jeffers, Susan. (1988) *Feel the Fear and Do It Anyway*. New York: Ballantine.

Kabat-Zinn, Jon. (1994) *Wherever You Go, There You Are*. New York: Hyperion.

Author Profile

Rosie Ross was born in Leigh, Lancashire in 1952. She attended secondary school in Bolton, then went to Durham University. Her career, though varied, was fuelled by a consistent desire to support people in finding their way. A qualified teacher, she worked in various fields of education until 2006, when she retrained as a psychotherapist. She retired in 2019. Rosie is a keen and eclectic musician and loves travel, walking and cycling.

She now lives in Lancaster. This is her first publication.

What Did You Think of

Rosie's Home! Positive Ageing for a Restless Spirit?

A big thank you for purchasing this book. It means a lot that you chose this book specifically from such a wide range on offer. I do hope you enjoyed it.

Book reviews are incredibly important for an author. If you are able to spare a few minutes to post a review on Amazon or elsewhere, that would be much appreciated.

Publisher Information

rowanvale
books

Rowanvale Books provides publishing services to independent authors, writers and poets all over the globe. We deliver a personal, honest and efficient service that allows authors to see their work published, while remaining in control of the process and retaining their creativity. By making publishing services available to authors in a cost-effective and ethical way, we at Rowanvale Books hope to ensure that the local, national and international community benefits from a steady stream of good quality literature.

For more information about us, our authors or our publications, please get in touch.

www.rowanvalebooks.com
info@rowanvalebooks.com